Music in Brazil

Music in Brazil

EXPERIENCING MUSIC,
EXPRESSING CULTURE

JOHN P. MURPHY

New York Oxford
Oxford University Press
2006

In memory of Gerard Béhague (1937–2005)

Oxford University Press, Inc., publishes works that further Oxford University's objective of excellence in research, scholarship, and education.

Oxford New York
Auckland Cape Town Dar es Salaam Hong Kong Karachi
Kuala Lumpur Madrid Melbourne Mexico City Nairobi
New Delhi Shanghai Taipei Toronto
With offices in
Argentina Austria Brazil Chile Czech Republic France Greece
Guatemala Hungary Italy Japan Poland Portugal Singapore
South Korea Switzerland Thailand Turkey Ukraine Vietnam

Published by Oxford University Press, Inc.
198 Madison Avenue, New York, New York 10016
www.oup.com

Library of Congress Cataloging-in-Publication Data
Murphy, John P. (John Patrick)
Music in Brazil : experiencing music, expressing culture / John P. Murphy.
p. cm. — (Global music series)
Includes bibliographical references (p.) and index.
ISBN-13: 978-0-19-516683-5 — ISBN-13: 978-0-19-516684-2 (pbk.)

1. Popular music—Brazil—History and criticism. 2. Folk music—Brazil—History and criticism. I. Title. II. Series.

ML3487.B7M85 2006
781.64'0981—dc22 2005049867

Printing number: 9 8 7 6 5 4 3 2

Printed in the United States of America
on acid-free paper

GLOBAL MUSIC SERIES

General Editors: Bonnie C. Wade and Patricia Shehan Campbell

Music in East Africa, by Gregory Barz
Music in Central Java, by Benjamin Brinner
Teaching Music Globally, by Patricia Shehan Campbell
Native American Music in Eastern North America, by Beverley Diamond
Carnival Music in Trinidad, by Shannon Dudley
Music in Bali, by Lisa Gold
Music in Ireland, by Dorothea E. Hast and Stanley Scott
Music in China, by Frederick Lau
Music in Egypt, by Scott Marcus
Music in Brazil, by John P. Murphy
Music in America, by Adelaida Reyes
Music in Bulgaria, by Timothy Rice
Music in North India, by George E. Ruckert
Mariachi Music in America, by Daniel Sheehy
Music in West Africa, by Ruth M. Stone
Music in the Andes, by Thomas Turino
Music in South India, by T. Viswanathan and Matthew Harp Allen
Music in Japan, by Bonnie C. Wade
Thinking Musically, by Bonnie C. Wade

Contents

Foreword xi
Preface xiii
CD Track List xvii

I MUSIC AND NATIONAL IDENTITY

1. **Samba, Brazil's National Music** 1
Carnaval in Recife: Traditional Musics and Current Pop in a Historic Setting 1
Samba in Rio de Janeiro: Music From the *Morros* 4
Varieties of Samba: Not Just for Carnaval 6
The History of Samba: From Marginal to National 7
Samba Percussion 10
The Malandro *and the* Mulata: *Samba and Gender Roles* 11
"The Mystery of Samba" 13
Carmen Miranda Brings the Samba to Hollywood 17
Samba and Carnaval: The Sambadrome and Beyond 19
Pagode 24
Samba Today: A Range of Meanings 26
Samba Raro 26
Eu Tiro é Onda 27
The Song "O Mistério do Samba" 27

2. Projecting Brazilian Identity Nationally and Internationally 29
Choro: An Early Rio de Janeiro Instrumental Style 29
The Emergence of Choro 30
Northeastern Influences 31
Pixinguinha 31
Jacob do Bandolim and Waldir Azevedo 33
The Choro *Revival* 33
Choro, Art Music, and Jazz 34
Women in Choro 34
Choro's *Current Vitality* 35
Brazilian Art Music Briefly Surveyed 35
Bossa nova: The Intimate Samba Sound Known Worldwide 36
The Term Bossa Nova 37
A Bossa Nova *Classic* 38
"The Girl from Ipanema" 38
Other Ways of Playing Bossa Nova 42
Bossa Nova *and Jazz* 44
The Sound of a Modernizing Brazil 44
Tropicália: Cultural Cannibalism, Late '60s Style 46
MPB: Sophisticated Songwriting With a Political Edge 48
Música Brega: Sentimental Songs Loved by Millions 50
The Romantic Balladry of Roberto Carlos 51

II MUSIC AND REGIONAL IDENTITY

3. Expressing Afro-Brazilian and Indigenous Identity 55
Capoeira: Music, Movement, and the Legacy of Zumbi 55
The Orquestra *and the* Berimbau 59
Capoeira: *Other American Martial Arts and the African Heritage* 61
Capoeira: *Resistance and Revolt* 62

Capoeira Regional *and* Atual 62
Music of Brazil's Indigenous Peoples 63
Music of the Kayapó-Kikrin: A Ritual of an Amazonian People 63
The Kayapó and the Environment 68
Inspired by Indigenous Music 69
Popular Music in the Amazon Region 70

4. The Sound of the Northeast 71
Bumba-meu-boi and *Cavalo-Marinho*: The Drama of the Magical Ox 71
Cavalo-marinho *Performers and Audiences* 73
Three Master Performers of Cavalo-marinho 73
Cavalo-marinho *Performance Contexts* 75
A Cavalo-marinho *Performance* 75
Cavalo-marinho *Today* 86
Maracatu: Afro-Brazilian Carnival Genre With a Sacred Side 86
A Sambada 87
Maracutu *Rural* 89
Siba and Barachinha's "Catimbó" 91
Baião and *Forró*: Accordion-Driven Dance Music 94
Luiz Gonzaga and the Baião 95
Luiz Gonzaga's Music and the Invention of the Northeast 99
Arlindo dos Oito Baixos and Instrumental Forró 100
The Technique of the Sanfona de Oito Baixos 104
The Symbolic Importance of the Sanfona de Oito Baixos 104
The Tune 105
Meter 106
Bellows 106
Rhythmic Accompaniment 107
Forró and Northeastern Identity 107

5. Expressing Southern Brazilian Identity 109
Música Caipira: Rural Music of the South 110
Música Caipira *in a Sacred Context:* Folias de Reis 111

Música Caipira *in a Secular Context* 113
Cantoria 113
Música Caipira *on Records and Radio* 113
The Viola Caipira 115
Roberto Corrêa and the *Viola Caipira* 116
Música Sertaneja: Brazilian "Country" Music 117
Música Gaúcha: Celebrating Brazil's Far South 121
The Nativist Movement in Rio Grande do Sul 122
Traditionalist *Música Gaúcha:* Leonardo 123
Renato Borghetti and Progressive Música Gaúcha 125
The Sound of the South 129
Popular Music and Social Action in Porto Alegre 129

III MUSICAL COSMOPOLITANISM

6. The Innovative Music and Scene of Recife 131
Brazilian Music and Cosmopolitanism 131
Cássia Eller 132
Tribalistas 132
Hermeto Pascoal 132
The *Mangue* Movement, Chico Science & Nação Zumbi, and Popular Music in Recife 133
Mundo Livre S/A: Working Toward a Free World 138
Devotos: A Hardcore Look at Life in Recife 144
Faces do Subúrbio: Rap and *Embolada* From the Alto José do Pinho 148
DJ Dolores e Orchestra Santa Massa: Electronic *Maracatu* 151
Comadre Florzinha and Women's Participation in the Recife Scene 156
Conclusion 158

Glossary 159
References 162
Resources 167
Index 170

Foreword

In the past three decades interest in music around the world has surged, as evidenced in the proliferation of courses at the college level, the burgeoning "world music" market in the recording business, and the extent to which musical performance is evoked as a lure in the international tourist industry. This heightened interest has encouraged an explosion in ethnomusicological research and publication, including the production of reference works and textbooks. The original model for the "world music" course—if this is Tuesday, this must be Japan—has grown old, as has the format of textbooks for it, either a series of articles in single multiauthored volumes that subscribe to the idea of "a survey" and have created a canon of cultures for study, or single-authored studies purporting to cover world musics or ethnomusicology. The time has come for a change.

This Global Music Series offers a new paradigm. Teachers can now design their own courses; choosing from a set of case study volumes, they can decide which and how many musics they will cover. The series also does something else; rather than uniformly taking a large region and giving superficial examples from several different countries within it, in some case studies authors have focused on a specific culture or a few countries within a larger region. Its length and approach permits each volume greater depth than the usual survey. Themes significant in each volume guide the choice of music that is discussed. The contemporary musical situation is the point of departure in all the volumes, with historical information and traditions covered as they elucidate the present. In addition, a set of unifying topics such as gender, globalization, and authenticity occur throughout the series. These are addressed in the framing volume, *Thinking Musically*, which sets the stage for the case studies by introducing ways to think about how people make music meaningful and useful in their lives and presenting basic musical concepts as they are practiced in musical systems around the world. A second framing volume, *Teaching Music Globally*, guides teachers in the use of *Thinking Musically* and the case studies.

The series subtitle, "Experiencing Music, Expressing Culture," also puts in the forefront the people who make music or in some other way experience it and also through it express shared culture. This resonance with global history studies, with their focus on processes and themes that permit cross-study, occasions the title of this Global Music Series.

Bonnie C. Wade
Patricia Shehan Campbell
General Editors

Preface

The music of Brazil is diverse and exciting. Little of it besides *samba* and *bossa nova*, however, is familiar to most people elsewhere. Like soccer and Carnaval, music animates the culture of Brazil, whose population, at 184 million, is the world's fifth largest. This book is intended to introduce students and other interested readers to Brazilian music through narratives of musical events, music history and analysis, the words of musicians and others involved in music, and explorations of the connections between music and other aspects of Brazilian culture and society.

Three themes organize the book. First, music and musical events express the unity of Brazilian culture by providing a focus for national identity. Illustrating that theme, Chapter 1 presents the history of samba, its role within Carnaval, the way it articulates concepts of gender and national identity, and some of its contemporary forms, whereas Chapter 2 describes five additional genres that project a national identity within Brazil and internationally: *choro*, an instrumental style closely associated with the beginnings of samba; *bossa nova*, with emphasis on the music of Antonio Carlos Jobim and João Gilberto; *Tropicália*, the brief yet influential pop movement of the late 1960s; *MPB (Música Popular Brasileira)*, a diverse category that includes the work of singers and composers of high artistic achivement; and the sentimental *brega* style of Roberto Carlos.

Secondly, music is an important way in which Brazilians express regional identity. Part II introduces readers to the diversity of regional musical styles in this huge country. Chapter 3 explores *capoeira*, the musical martial art that is strongly associated with the Northeast and has found adherents around the world, and the music of the Kayapó-Kikrin of the Amazonian region. Chapter 4 discusses *cavalo-marinho*, a folk musical drama that is a regional variant of the well-known *bumba-meu-boi; maracatu*, an Afro-Brazilian musical and poetic tradition; and the *baião* as exemplified by the work of Luiz Gonzaga and the associated *forró* style. Chapter 5 focuses on *música caipira*, the folk music of the interior of South-Central Brazil; *música sertaneja*, popular vocal duos that developed from traditional *caipira* genres; and *música gaúcha*, the music of the far South region of the country.

Third, Brazilian musicians and listeners demonstrate *cosmopolitanism* by participating in genres that can be considered global, such as rock, rap, and electronica. Part III (Chapter 6) shows how Brazilian musicians have adapted global styles to communicate a Brazilian worldview, with emphasis on the popular music scene of Recife.

The themes of national identity, regional identity, and cosmopolitanism provide a way to categorize music. But it would also be possible to discuss each genre in terms of all three themes. *Bossa nova*, for example, which I present as an expression of national identity and of Brazil's modernization during the 1950s, can also be heard as a sign of the cosmopolitanism of the Rio de Janeiro music scene of those years. *Capoeira*, presented here as a regional tradition associated with Afro-Brazilian culture in Bahia, can be understood as a cosmopolitan, transnational style that combines ancient moves of African origin with the practices of Asian martial arts. The music of DJ Dolores, presented as an example of cosmopolitanism, draws on the regional *maracatu* tradition of Pernambuco state. This complex interweaving of national, regional, and cosmopolitan strands is part of what makes Brazilian music so exhilarating and intriguing.

One of the most distinctive aspects of Brazilian music is the sound of the Portuguese language. All six chapters include song texts, musical terms, and everyday expressions in Portuguese, along with translations, so that a non-Portuguese speaking reader can begin to appreciate the subtleties of this very musical language. Suggestions for pronunciation may be found on my website, which is linked to the site for this series, ⟨www.oup.com/us/globalmusic⟩. Whenever the text refers to the web site without further explanation, this is the site intended.

I think of this book as an interface to Brazilian music, a simplified structure that hides a complex reality. Like a software interface, it may contain more options than a typical reader might use. I have included the names of many musicians and the titles of many recordings, films, and publications so that readers can continue to investigate Brazilian music independently. In many cases I decided to include the name of a significant musician, even when space limitations prevented a full discussion, in order to enable readers to search for information, sound clips, and images related to that artist on the Web. I will assist with that by posting supplementary and updated information on my web site as well.

Given the very broad scope of Brazilian music, it is important to acknowledge my limitations as a guide. I came to enjoy and study Brazilian music after studying and performing jazz and many kinds of U.S. popular music and researching Cuban music in New York. My initial research interests led me to concentrate on the music and culture of Northeast Brazil. With my family, I spent two years in Recife, first in 1990–1991 and again in 2000–2001, so many of my examples will rely on experiences I had there. On those visits and several shorter ones, including trips to other parts of the country, I have experienced a broad range of music as part of my ongoing research on Brazilian music, as preparation for writing this book, and for personal enjoyment. Nevertheless, there are many kinds of Brazilian music that I have yet to explore.

Like other authors in this series, I have found the cost of obtaining the rights to reproduce many of the musical works mentioned in this book to be prohibitive. Fortunately, CDs by many of the artists mentioned are readily available, as are CD compilations. These are noted in the text, in the resources section, and on my web site, which will link to online excerpts when they are legally available.

Finally, my relationship with Brazilian music has been motivated by a strong attachment not only to the music but also to Brazilians themselves, individually and collectively. This book expresses my gratitude for the way experiencing Brazilian music and culture has enriched my life.

ACKNOWLEDGMENTS

Many people made this book and the research that supports it possible. I am grateful to Bonnie Wade and Patricia Sheehan Campbell for the invitation to contribute to this series; to Jan Beatty, Talia Krohn, Lisa Grzan, and the rest of the editorial and production team at Oxford University Press for their highly competent work; and to the reviewers Philip Galinsky, University of California, Davis, Matthew Allen, Wheaton College, and Ricardo Lorenz, Indiana University, for many valuable suggestions.

For major research funding, I owe a debt of gratitude to the U.S. Dept. of Education for a Fulbright-Hays Doctoral Dissertation Research Abroad Fellowship in 1990–91; to the Mrs. Giles Whiting Foundation for a Fellowship in the Humanities that supported dissertation writing in 1991–1992; and to the National Endowment for the Humanities for a research fellowship in 2000–2001. Malena Kuss and Gene Cho at the University of North Texas introduced me to ethnomusicology. At Columbia University, I benefited from Dieter Christensen's counsel during dissertation research and writing and from classes with him and the rest of the ethnomusicology faculty, and Irwin Stern and Vasda Landers gave me a solid foundation in Portuguese. In Brazil, Peggy Sharpe, Esman Dias, and countless conversation partners helped me refine my language skills. My two employers, the University of North Texas and Western Illinois University, provided a variety of research support. The Universidade Federal de Pernambuco was an institutional home base during both of my years in Recife, and during the latter one Carlos Sandroni and the students in the ethnomusicology program welcomed me into their community. At the Universidade de São Paulo, Flávia Toni was my guide to the Mário de Andrade archives.

For research relationships that have grown into long-term friendships, I am grateful to Siba and to Sérgio Gusmão. I thank Mestre Salustiano, the late Mestre Batista, and Mestre Inácio, my professors of cavalo-marinho, and Arlindo dos Oito Baixos, my accordion teacher, for their wisdom and patience. Larry Crook gave me an early introduction to Recife; he and Charles Perrone, Philip Galinsky, and Suzel Ana Reily have been supportive colleagues. In Recife, Renato L., Fred04, José Teles, and Elcy Oliveira have been especially generous with their expertise.

I am grateful to my parents, Charles and Angela Murphy, for their love and support, and to my wife, Genene, and children, Jack, Peter, and Gillian, for accompanying me to Brazil and for graciously tolerating my attention divided between home and work.

I'd like to express my gratitude to all of the musicians, authors, and photographers on whose work I drew in this volume, to all of the supportive friends whom I was unable to mention here, and to Brazilian musicians in general for the music they've given the world.

CD Track List

1. "Língua de Preto" (2:59) by Honorino Lopes. From the recording entitled *Henrique Cazes* (MusiCazes LPMCZ 001, 1988). Henrique Cazes (*cavaquinho, viola,* arrangement), Rafael Rabello (7-string *viola*), Luiz Otávio Braga (*violão*), Beto Cazes (*pandeiro, adufe,* wood-*agogô*). Used by permission.
2. "Rei Zumbi Dos Palmares" (1:34). From the recording entitled *Capoeira Angola from Salvador, Brazil,* 40465, provided courtesy of Smithsonian Folkways Recordings. © 1996. Used by permission.
3. "Chula" (0:45). From the recording entitled *Capoeira Angola from Salvador, Brazil,* SF 40465, provided courtesy of Smithsonian Folkways Recordings. © 1996. Used by permission.
4. "Santa Bárbara" (1:23). From the recording entitled *Capoeira Angola from Salvador, Brazil,* SF 40465, provided courtesy of Smithsonian Folkways Recordings. © 1996. Used by permission.
5. "Angola" (2:24). From the recording entitled *Capoeira Angola from Salvador, Brazil,* SF 40465, provided courtesy of Smithsonian Folkways Recordings. © 1996. Used by permission.
6. "Nhiok: Okkaikrikti" (2:10). From the recording entitled *Traditional Music of the World Vol. 7: Ritual Music of the Kayapó-Xikrin, Brazil,* Smithsonian Folkways 40433, provided courtesy of Smithsonian Folkways Recordings. © 1995. Used by permission.
7. "Que estrela é aquela" (1:11). *Cavalo-Marinho* of Inácio Lucindo da Silva. Field recording by J. Murphy, 1991.
8. "Inácio's toada" (0:58). *Cavalo-Marinho* of Inácio Lucindo da Silva. Field recording by J. Murphy, 1991.
9. "Rabeca baianos" (3:18). *Cavalo-Marinho* of Inácio Lucindo da Silva. Field recording by J. Murphy, 1991.
10. "Boi toada" (0:48). *Cavalo-Marinho* of Inácio Lucindo da Silva. Field recording by J. Murphy, 1991.
11. "Boi toada" (3:14). *Cavalo-Marinho* of Mestre Batista. Field recording by J. Murphy, 1991.
12. "Catimbó" (7:17). From the recording entitled *No baque solto somente* by Siba and Barachinha. Terreiro Discos TDCD 054. © 2003. Siba and Barachinha (voice and *apito*), Biu Roque (*bombo* and chorus), Mané Roque (chorus), Cosme Antônio (*tarol* and chorus), Zeca (*gongué*), Mané Martins (*póica*), Dachinha (*mineiro*), Dyógenes Santos (trombone), Galego (trombone), Roberto Manoel (trumpet). Used by permission.

13. "Forró em Monteiro" (0:55) by Arlindo dos Oito Baixos. Arlindo dos Oito Baixos (*sanfona de oito baixos*). Field recording by J. Murphy, 2001.
14. "Forró em Monteiro" (1:34) by Arlindo dos Oito Baixos. Arlindo dos Oito Baixos (*sanfona de oito baixos*), Raminho (*zabumba*), Adilson (bass). Field recording by J. Murphy, 2001.
15. "Queluzindo" (3:17) by Roberto Corrêa. From the recording entitled *Extremosa-Rosa* by Roberto Corrêa. Roberto Corrêa (*viola*). Viola Corrêa Produções Artísticas VC-04. © 2001. Used by permission.
16. "Céu, Sol, Sul, Terra e Cor" (excerpt, 2:57) by Leonardo. From the recording *Só Sucessos* by Leonardo. Leonardo (vocal), Cristiano Teixeira (drums and percussion), Régis Marques (accordion), Marli, Mirian, Cristiano, Oscar, and Leonardo (backing vocals), Oscar Soares (guitars, *cavaquinho*, bass, arrangement). USA Discos. © 2001. Used by permission.
17. "Milonga Para as Missões" (3:14) by Gilberto Monteiro. From the recording entitled *Gauderiando* by Renato Borghetti. Renato Borghetti (*gaita-ponto*), Kiko Freitas (drums), Renato Mujeiko (bass), Daniel Sá (acoustic and electric guitars), Giovani Berti (*congas*, cowbell, *xequerê, djembe*), Fernando do Ó (*congas, caxixi, xequerê*, cowbell, *surdo, congô*), Jorginho do Trompete (trumpet), Pedro Figueiredo (soprano and tenor saxophone, flute, arrangement). © 2003. Used by permission.
18. "O Outro Mundo de Xicão Xukuru" (5:33). Lyrics by Fred04. Music by Fred04, Bac, Tony, Areia, Marcelo Pianinho, and Fábio Goró. From the recording *O Outro Mundo de Manuela Rosário* by Mundo Livre S/A. Candeeiro Records ⟨www.candeeiro.com.br⟩. © 2003. Used by permission.
19. "Meu País" (4:51). Lyrics by Cannibal. Music by Devotos. From the recording *Devotos* by Devotos. Cannibal (bass and voice), Toni Platão (voice), Neilton (*guitarra, violão*), Dado Villa-Lobos (guitarra, *violão, ebow*), Celo Brown (drums), Wally (piano). Rockit! R!-021. © 2000. Used by permission.
20. "Perito em Rima" (3:55) by Faces do Subúrbio. From the recording *Perito em Rima* by Faces do Subúrbio. © 2005. Used by permission.
21. "Samba de Dez Linhas" (5:43) by Maciel Salustiano. From the recording *Contraditório?* by DJ Dolores e Orchestra Santa Massa. MC Salu (*rabeca*, voice), Fábio Trummer (*guitarra*), Karina Buhr and Isaar França (chorus), Nilsinho (trombone), DJ Dolores (programming). Candeeiro T005/602–2. © 2002. Used by permission.

CHAPTER 1

Samba, Brazil's National Music

CARNAVAL IN RECIFE: TRADITIONAL MUSICS AND CURRENT POP IN A HISTORIC SETTING

It is Monday night of Carnaval, and the streets of Old Recife, on Brazil's Northeast coast (see map of Brazil, Figure 1.1), are filled with people. The narrow cobblestoned streets echo with a syncopated pattern on deep bass drums, its gaps filled by snare drum and two-pitched metal bell, which signals the presence of a *maracatu de baque virado*, a Carnaval group that resembles an Afro-Brazilian royal procession. Around the next corner, just off the Rua do Bom Jesus (Good Jesus Street), which used to be called the Rua dos Judeus (Street of the Jews), site of the first synagogue in the New World, near a crowded sidewalk café, a *frevo* orchestra has paused to play. Its trumpets, trombones, saxophones, and clarinets play a jaunty march while onlookers try a few steps of the *frevo*, a dance full of deep knee-bends, kicks, and whirls. A loud metallic clanking signals the presence of a *maracatu de baque solto*, a mock warlike Carnaval group whose costumes blend Afro-Brazilian and Indian styles, and its most colorful and fearsome figure, the *caboclo de lança*, a man wearing an enormous cape decorated with multicolored sequins, a tall hat with thousands of multicolored streamers, a long spear similarly decorated, a rack of large cowbells on his back, and a white flower clutched in his teeth (Figure 1.2).

A few blocks away, thousands of young people have crammed into the Rua da Moeda (Mint Street) in front of a stage that closes off one end of the street to hear an eclectic mix of rock, rap, funk, and traditional bands. This is Rec-Beat, a festival of popular music that happens during Carnaval. And on the large stage at Marco Zero (the zero mark from which distances are measured), an *escola de samba* (samba school) shakes the windows of nearby buildings with the sound of its *bateria* (percussion ensemble).

FIGURE 1.1 *Map of Brazil*

Old Recife, a narrow coastal island linked by bridges to the rest of the city, is the site of the city's first port area and business district. Until recently it was a business district by day, with offices of major banks, government offices, and businesses supporting the port; by night it was mostly deserted and given over to unsavory activities. During the 1990s, however, young people started renting loft spaces for dance parties, and a nightlife scene developed. Now the city has renovated many of the colonial buildings. There are restaurants, theatres, and nightclubs; the city and local arts groups regularly sponsor outdoor concerts, including those that happen during Carnaval; and beneath the streets runs a

FIGURE 1.2 Caboclos-de-lança *parade during Carnaval in Recife. Inset: close-up of an unidentified* caboclo-de-lança. *Photos by Sérgio Gusmão.* (*Used by permission.*)

network of fiber-optic cables, part of the Digital Port initiative aimed at attracting high-tech businesses to the area.

All sorts of people have come out for Carnaval in Old Recife: groups of young people, families with small children, older people; some in costume, others not; people are in a festive mood, but few seem intoxicated; there are police around, and the papers will have stories on robberies after Carnaval is over, but for now the crowd seems tranquil.

Up the Atlantic coast a few miles lies Olinda, one of the oldest cities in Brazil. Its steep, narrow streets are also packed with *frevo* bands, *maracatu* groups, and gigantic puppets. Crowds of giddy young people in costume careen through the streets, shooting each other with squirt guns full of dirty water.

In the Recife city center, church plazas host *maracatu* competitions and samba school parades. A huge daytime gathering called the Galo da Madrugada attracts perhaps a million people to the downtown area to kick off the final three days of Carnaval, which culminate many weeks of anticipatory celebrations. The streets are filled with *frevo* groups and folkloric groups including *Caboclinhos*, who dress as Indians and play flute and drums, and *Bois de Carnaval*, magical oxen accompanied by herdsmen, Indian shamans, and clowns. In outlying neighborhoods, rock bands and all of the Carnaval groups mentioned so far perform on city-sponsored stages.

If one knew only what was reported by the media outside Brazil, one might think of Carnaval only as it is practiced in Rio de Janeiro. While Rio is indeed the center of the Carnaval universe, Carnaval is celebrated all over Brazil in various ways. Salvador, in Bahia state, has its own distinctive Carnaval music, including *blocos afro* playing a samba-reggae rhythm, and high-energy pop music called *axé* played and sung by performers atop huge sound trucks. São Paulo, the largest city in Brazil and one of the largest in the world, has parades of *escolas de samba* as well.

What is common to all of these celebrations, and what makes Carnaval an expression of Brazilianness, is the joyous energy that people put into them. Whether one is a day-laborer who plays percussion in an *escola de samba*, a rich person who attends an elaborate costume ball, a teenager who follows behind a *trio elétrico*, a professional parading with a group of friends from the office, or someone who stays home and watches it all on TV, Carnaval provides a chance to step outside of everyday routines and dissolve the cares and frustrations of the previous year in musical revelry.

Music expresses the unity of Brazilian culture by providing a focus for national identity. Part I of this book presents music that is either officially regarded as a symbol of national identity or has such a large national audience that it can be said to articulate a national sentiment. In Chapter 1, I concentrate on Carnaval and samba, the music most closely associated with it. In Chapter 2, I discuss music that has projected Brazil's identity both nationally and internationally: *choro*, Brazilian art music, *bossa nova*, *MPB* (*Música popular brasileira*), *Tropicália*, and the sentimental pop style of Roberto Carlos that is sometimes labeled *brega*.

SAMBA IN RIO DE JANEIRO: MUSIC FROM THE *MORROS*

During Carnaval in Rio de Janeiro, the parade of samba schools (*escolas de samba*) fills the Sambadrome (*Sambódromo*), a stadium constructed

FIGURE 1.3 Escola de samba *in the* Sambódromo. *(Photo courtesy Contéudo Expresso, www.contentxp.com.)*

just for this purpose, with hundreds of brightly costumed dancers and musicians and the towering floats (*carros alegóricos*, or trucks that carry the allegorical displays) that embody each samba school's theme (Figure 1.3). On street level, women whose costumes include long dresses, tall decorative hats, and glittery makeup, move in stately swirls; men in sparkling formal attire carrying jewel-encrusted canes jauntily accompany them; slim women wearing skimpy, shiny bikinis, high heels, and feathered masks or headdresses, their sweat shining through their makeup, swivel their hips rapidly and gracefully while bare-chested male dancers circulate among them. High on the floats are even more elaborately costumed dancers, their dance steps confined to a small platform, some of them celebrities whose job is to wave and smile for the cameras that will send this spectacle to every corner of Brazil on network television. And the musicians, hundreds of them, wear brightly colored costumes and play an array of percussion instruments that covers the spectrum, from low (the *surdo* drum) through the middle register occupied by the friction drum (*cuíca*) and the snare drum (*caixa*) to the highest-pitched instrument, the six-inch drum (*tamborim*). A group of guitars (*violões*) and small guitars, called *cavaquinho*, provide a harmonic accompaniment for the singers who lead the chorus in this year's theme song (*samba-enredo*), which conveys the same theme that is portrayed visually in the *carro alegórico* and the costumes. Cutting through it all is the amplified voice that announces the name of the *escola de samba*, and shining down on it all are banks of strong lights that play off of the millions of tiny mirrors sewn into the costumes.

ACTIVITY 1.1 *Find Rio de Janeiro and the following cities on the map of Brazil (see Figure 1.1): São Paulo, Brasília (the capital), Salvador, Recife, Belo Horizonte, Porto Alegre, Manaus, Belém. Review also the names of the states.*

VARIETIES OF SAMBA: NOT JUST FOR CARNAVAL

There are many kinds of samba besides Carnaval samba. Sambas are sung by solo singers in a nightclub or concert setting, with accompaniments ranging from guitar to full orchestra. In the traditional *samba-de-roda* of Bahia, dancers accompanied by percussion take turns entering the ring formed by musicians, other dancers, and onlookers. Sambas have been arranged for every type of group from big band to orchestra. Samba's subtle 1950s offshoot, *bossa nova*, became an internationally known genre. Alternative rock bands play sambas with sarcastic or political lyrics. Samba samples are mixed with *electrônica* dance beats. Which is the "authentic" samba? It is tempting to pick one style, such as that of the Velha Guarda da Mangueira, which performs classic sambas of the early twentieth century, and call it *the* authentic style and the others adaptations or distortions. But this would itself be a distortion of an important quality of samba: it is as multi-faceted and adaptable as the Brazilian people themselves.

A better answer would be to recognize samba not as a single genre or style but as a broad stream of musical activity comparable to jazz. The parallels between samba and jazz are many, and for good reason: the early twentieth century was a time when European-derived dance musics were being combined with African-derived musical practices, and urban and rural musical traditions were being blended in many places in the Americas as cities and their respective musical cultures grew rapidly. At the same time, the new technologies of records and radio made the new sounds available to a mass audience. The recordings that scholars recognize as the first in each style were made in 1917: "Pelo Telofone," by Donga and Mauro de Almeida, and "Livery Stable Blues," by the Original Dixieland Jazz Band. Both samba and jazz emerged from the blending of strongly African ways of making music with European-derived harmonies, instruments, and musical forms; both are strongly associated with dance; both became symbols of national identity after being subjected to criticism by musical elitists for their association with less respectable segments of society; both involve improvisatory playing and singing; both have become global styles; both encompass multiple substyles that use a variety of instrumentations; both are urban styles that include rural traditions in their source styles; both originated in cities with an especially intense musical life (Rio de Janeiro and New Orleans); both involve a strong pulse with layers of contrasting rhythms. The list could go on. One might argue further that Brazilian music is part of the mix of styles from which jazz originated—since James Reese Europe, who led an important dance orchestra in New York and a military band during World War I, recorded a Brazilian *maxixe* and an Argentine *tango* in 1913. The larger point is that samba and jazz refer to a family of styles, not a single style. For jazz, this includes New Orleans traditional style, big band swing, bebop, and so on. For samba, this includes Carnaval samba (*samba-enredo*), *samba-canção*, *pagode*, and many other styles.

THE HISTORY OF SAMBA: FROM MARGINAL TO NATIONAL

The urban samba of Rio de Janeiro developed from traditional forms of samba that had been practiced in the Northeast region, especially Bahia state, which scholars link to the Congo-Angola region of Africa. They were brought to Rio de Janeiro during a post-emancipation wave of labor migration in the late nineteenth century. Musical occasions and the dance and music associated with them were known as *batuque*. The dances included the *umbigada*, a movement in which a pair of dancers touched their navels together. The houses of Bahian women such as Tia Ciata (Hilária Batista de Almeida, 1854–1924) in the Praça Onze section of Rio de Janeiro became centers of musical and religious activity in the early decades of the twentieth century.

Bahian migrants and their children gathered there for observances of *candomblé*, the Afro-Brazilian religion in which participants cultivate a personal relationship with a pantheon of deities called *orixás* by means of spirit possession. Like Cuban *santería* and Haitian *vodun*, *candomblé* features call-and-response singing to the accompaniment of multiple drums and metal bell. *Candomblé* and related spiritual practices were subject to repression through approximately the mid-twentieth century. Since the 1950s, it has become more publicly acknowledged and accepted, and is practiced by Brazilians of all racial and ethnic heritages. There are complex relationships between *candomblé* and various forms of Brazilian popular music, especially in Bahia, and the names of *orixás* appear in many song lyrics. Leci Brandão's "Saudação a Ossain," for example, which is included on *The Rough Guide to Samba* [2001]—hereafter abbreviated *RGS*—features percussion in *candomblé* style.

Listening to Samba. *When I was successful in licensing music for the CD that accompanies this book, it was usually due to personal contacts with artists. Lacking such contacts in the world of samba artists, record companies, and publishers, I was unsuccessful. Fortunately, samba compilations are plentiful and easily available. Use the list of samba compilation CDs, videos, and web sites in the resources section to find examples of the varieties of samba described in this chapter.*

The early Bahian migrants to Rio de Janeiro also had informal music sessions during which the dance genres that were popular at the time, including the *lundu*, *maxixe*, and polka, were blended with the syncopated and percussive religious music by musicians including Donga (Ernesto Joaquim Maria dos Santos, 1888–1974), Sinhô (José Barbosa da Silva, 1888–1930), João da Baiana (João Machado Guedes, 1887–1974), Heitor dos Prazeres (1898–1966), and Pixinguinha (Alfredo da Rocha

Viana Filho, 1897–1973). The first recorded samba, "Pelo Telefone" ("On the Telephone," Donga and Mauro de Almeida, 1917), is a product of this musical community. Both the authorship of this piece (claimed by Donga alone) and its correct musical style label have been the subject of controversy. Despite the spoken identification of "samba carnavalesco" (Carnival samba) at the beginning of the recording, it is closer to the *maxixe*, which combined elements of the tango and the polka. The rhythm of sixteenth-eighth-sixteenth, followed by two eighths, a variant of the *habanera* rhythm (dotted eighth, sixteenth, two eighths), is prominent in the accompaniment of the original recorded version, and the tempo is a relaxed 76–80 bpm (counted in 2/4). *RGS* includes an instrumental version of this song by clarinetist Paulo Moura.

The circle of musicians of the *morros*, or poorer hillside sections of the Estácio de Sá neighborhood, played an important role in the development of samba in the late 1920s. In earlier years, Carnaval groups called *ranchos* would parade together accompanied by *marchas* (marches). In 1928, the first *escola de samba*, Deixa Falar, was formed. According to Allison Raphael,

> As legend has it, they called themselves a "Samba School" because their headquarters was located across the dirt lane from the neighborhood primary school and because they were proud to proclaim that they were the teachers of samba (1990: 75).

The samba school label and the school's name, which means roughly "Let them speak," were also signs of resistance to the oppression of samba musicians by local authorities and disapproval by the middle class (Tinhorão 1998: 292–3). In order to coordinate the tempo of a large group of dancers and musicians, the musician Bide (Alcebíades Maia Barcelos, 1902–1975) introduced the practice of playing the second beat of a 2/4 measure strongly on the *surdo* bass drum and using the *tamborim* in the samba percussion section (Tinhorão 1998: 293–94; Souza et al. 1988: 147). The composers of the Estácio neighborhood, including Ismael Silva (1905–1978), made important contributions to the samba style and repertory with a style that became known as *samba de morro*, after the hillside neighborhoods.

> They took the fledgling samba genre and clearly differentiated it from maxixe and marcha, introducing longer notes and two-bar phrasing, and making the tempo slower, in contrast to the maxixe-like sambas composed by Sinhô and Donga. The form they codified became the standard reference of samba, to which sambistas always return. (McGowan and Pessanha 1998: 25).

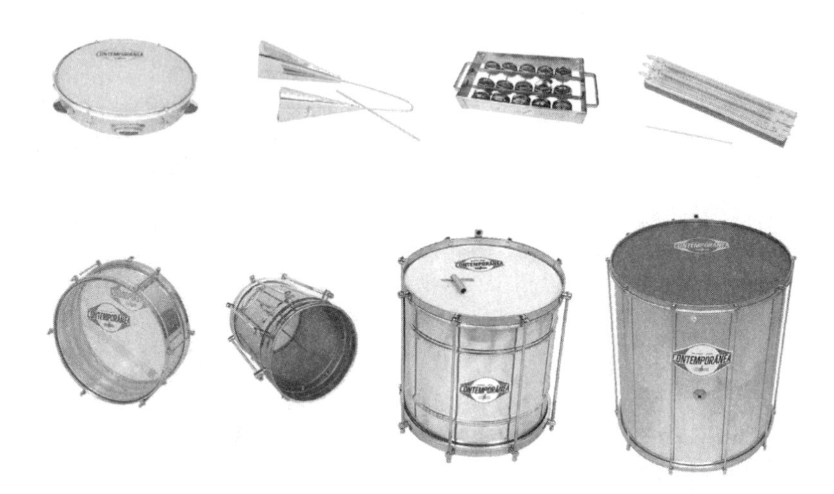

FIGURES 1.4 AND 1.5 *Samba percussion instruments. Top, left to right: pandeiro, agogô, ganzá, reco-reco. Bottom, left to right: caixa, cuíca, repinque, surdo. (Photos by Celia Dias, courtesy Contemporânea and Todd Steinkamp of Spanway Imports [brazil-drums.com]. Used by permission.)*

Because this style formed the basis for the style of samba played by the samba schools, I'll make a pause in the narrative in order to present a model of the contemporary form of that style.

Samba Percussion. The samba rhythm is played by the samba school's percussion section, which is called the *bateria*. The basic patterns played by the instruments in the *bateria* were generously provided by Jonathan Gregory, an experienced percussionist from Rio de Janeiro who is currently a student at the University of North Texas. He has performed with the samba schools Acadêmicos de Grande Rio, Acadêmicos da Rocinha, and Unidos da Tijuca and with the percussion group Monobloco and is the author of a forthcoming method for *pandeiro*.

The sixteenth notes are not even, but are given a special "swing," a term that Brazilian musicians have Brazilianized as *suingue*. Jonathan Gregory, who has made precise measurements of the time placement of *pandeiro* strokes, explains it as a slight delay of the second sixteenth note of the four-sixteenth note group. The amount of delay and the subsequent acceleration of the remaining notes are highly individual and varied. Gregory suggests the following as a way to approximate this ef-

FIGURE 1.6 *Samba percussion patterns.*

fect: play two against three as shown in Figure 1.8a, which produces a total of five attacks per beat. To make this playable in a R-L-R-L drumming pattern, omit the first note of the part that is playing in two, as shown in Figure 1.8b. The result will be a pattern of four sixteenth notes with a delay before the second note, as suggested by the spacing in Figure 1.8c.

The Malandro *and the* Mulata: *Samba and Gender Roles.* Samba lyricists of the 1920s through the 1950s established a recurring theme: relationships between men and women as they are affected by work

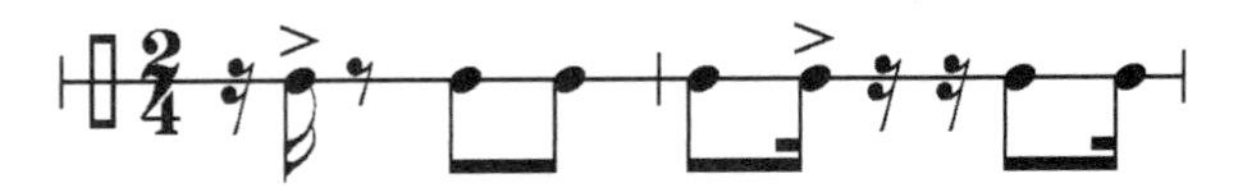

FIGURE 1.7 *Samba pattern for pandeiro. Key: L/ = low muffled (stopped or closed); F = finger; P = palm; L = low; Lmf = low open tone with middle finger*

and money. Appearing prominently in lyrics of this period is the figure of the *malandro*, the slick urban hipster who lives by his wits at the expense of others, a lifestyle and behavior called *malandragem*. Musicologist Carlos Sandroni argues that the change in the style of samba by the Estácio composers is related to the theme of *malandragem* (2001). He identifies two recurring themes in sambas of the late 1920s and early 1930s: the protagonist who debates whether to leave the promiscuous *malandro* lifestyle for a settled one of true love, and the protagonist who contemplates leaving that lifestyle for an honest job.

An analysis of gender roles in samba lyrics of the 1930s, 1940s, and 1950s by anthropologist Ruben George Oliven (1988) shows how women are represented as sources of domestic security or as seductresses who always bring with them the possibility of betrayal. In the classic samba "Ai Que Saudades da Amélia" (Ah, How I Miss Amélia, 1942) by Ataulfo Alves and Mário Lago, the narrator complains about his current partner, who demands luxuries he cannot provide, and the departed Amélia, who didn't mind being poor and hungry. The song ends, "Amélia wasn't vain at all/Amélia was a real woman." Tellingly, the real Amélia worked as a domestic servant for a friend of Mário Lago, the lyricist (Severiano and Homem de Mello 2002 I:205). *Saudade* (longing) is often cited as a distinctively Brazilian emotion, and it appears in countless song lyrics. Sambas inspired by betrayal are exemplified by "Nervos de Aço" (Nerves of Steel, 1947) and "Vingança" (Vengeance,

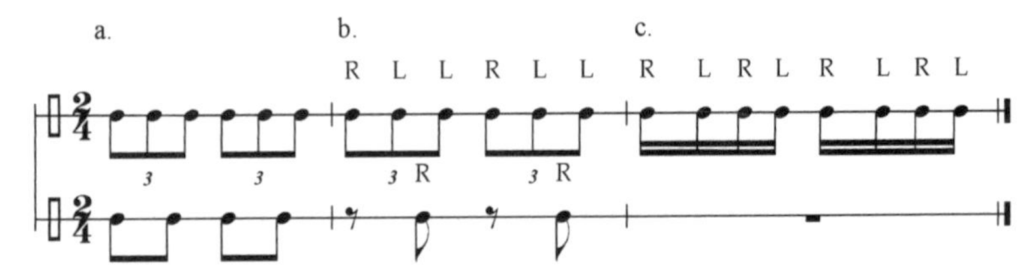

FIGURE 1.8 *Sixteenth notes with* suingue.

1951) by Lupicínio Rodrigues. In the former song, the narrator admits to not having the nerves of steel that would enable him to withstand the pain of betrayal; in the latter, the narrator revels in news of the misfortune that has befallen his unfaithful lover.

The *mulata*, the attractive mixed-race woman who is so prominently featured in *escolas de samba*, in stage shows, and in the image of Brazil that is projected abroad, is a complex cultural figure, as Gilliam and Gilliam explain (1999). They relate the *mulata* to the legacy of the colonial plantation economy, which created distinct roles of marriage, pleasure, and work for white, mulatto, and black women, respectively, and explain how hair type can be as complex a marker of race as skin color. Like seemingly everything else in Brazilian culture, this is reflected in samba lyrics, as in the song "Nega do Cabelo Duro" (*Black Woman with the Hard Hair*, by Rubens Soares and David Nasser), which mocks the practice of straightening hair with a hot comb. In the words of Gilliam and Gilliam,

> Applying a hot comb to the hair to remove the waves or kinks has been a very common practice of black women throughout the hemisphere. The words to the song, written in 1940, manifest the marginalization of the black woman in Brazil, and the fact that it remains one of the most popular and durable of sambas reinforces the social distance (1999: 71).

Angela Gilliam conducted anthropological research in the 1970s, during Brazil's years of military dictatorship. Her public comments about the existence of racism were controversial because they conflicted with Brazilian national myths about its absence.

"The Mystery of Samba." Ethnomusicologist Hermano Vianna has called attention to an important shift in the perception of samba, from the persecuted music of the mostly Afro-Brazilian underclass to a symbol of Brazilianness. He calls this gap between two moments in the history of samba "the mystery of samba":

> The first moment is the repression of samba, a time when the music was sequestered in the favelas of Rio, limited to the "popular classes." In the second moment, the sambistas triumph in carnival and on the radio, becoming symbols of Brazil as a whole, establishing relationships with all sectors of Brazilian society, constituting a new image of the country intended for both internal and international consumption (1999: 10).

In his book of the same title, Vianna shows how the change in the status of the samba is part of a broader shift in Brazilian national consciousness that included a new appreciation for Afro-Brazilian culture as essentially Brazilian and a new positive view of race-mixing, which Brazilian intellectuals of previous generations had viewed negatively as a reason for Brazil's perceived backwardness. He identifies an evening of samba in 1926 as a crucial meeting of samba musicians and intellectuals. Gilberto Freyre, the sociologist from Recife who would later write *The Masters and the Slaves,* which changed the way Brazilians regarded their Afro-Brazilian heritage, was visiting Rio de Janeiro for the first time after having attended Baylor University and Columbia University, where he studied anthropology with Franz Boas. He was invited to accompany historian Sérgio Buarque de Holanda, who later wrote *Roots of Brazil,* Rio district attorney and journalist Pedro Dantas Prudente de Moraes Neto, and composers Heitor Villa-Lobos and Luciano Gallet for an evening of music by the sambistas Patrício, Donga, and Pixinguinha (Vianna 1999: 1–2). Freyre wrote that this evening of music helped him to realize that Brazilians should stop trying to imitate European cultural models and instead should look for their national identity in Afro-Brazilian culture, especially music. In Freyre's words, "black song forms, black dances, mixed with traces of *fado* [a Portuguese genre with Brazilian roots] . . . are perhaps the best thing Brazil has to offer" (quoted in Vianna 1999: 9).

The 1926 encounter between intellectuals and samba musicians is representative of a major shift in the Brazilian national self-image that occurred in the 1920s and 1930s, a time when many countries were looking to their own people and culture as a source of identity rather than continuing to use the culture of the leading European nations as the unquestioned criterion. In Cuba, for example, the scholarship of Fernando Ortiz helped to raise awareness of the value of Afro-Cuban musical traditions (see Moore 1997 and Hagedorn 2001).

Three events, which are part of Brazilian artistic Modernism, symbolize this shift in Brazilian national identity: the *Semana de Arte Moderna* (Modern Art Week) was held in São Paulo in 1922, one hundred years after Dom Pedro I declared Brazil's independence from Portugal. An expression of cultural nationalism, it involved important figures in all of the arts, including writers Oswald de Andrade and Mário de Andrade (no relation), composer Heitor Villa-Lobos, and painter Anita Malfatti (Dunn 2001: 14). The second event is the publication in 1928 of Oswald de Andrade's "Manifesto Antropofágico" (Cannibalist Manifesto), the second of two statements of poetic principles, which advocated a sort of cultural cannibalism through which Brazilian artists would take in a diverse set of influences, digest them, and produce a fusion that was uniquely Brazilian (Dunn 2001: 19). This publication has inspired a literature of its own and provided the inspiration for numerous artistic experiments since, including the *Tropicália* movement of the 1960s. The third event is the publication, also in 1928, of two important works by Mário de Andrade, the musicologist and literary figure. His novel *Macunaíma* drew on Native Brazilian mythology to construct an allegory of Brazilian racial identity and progress. His *Ensaio Sobre a Música Brasileira* (Essay on Brazilian Music) urged composers to seek inspiration in Brazilian folk music rather than in European art music. Using "race" in the sense of the Brazilian people as a whole, he wrote, "Brazilian popular music is the most complete, most totally national, most powerful creation of our race so far" (quoted in Dunn 2001: 23). Mário de Andrade also made an important study of the samba in rural São Paulo state.

The political context for artistic Modernism is the use of folk and popular music as a marker of Brazilian national identity that was advocated during the regime of Getúlio Vargas (1883–1954). A former governor of Rio Grande do Sul, he led the revolution of 1930 with support from the military after failing to be elected president. He established the *Estado Novo*, a period of dictatorship, in 1937 and continued to lead an authoritarian government until he was removed from power by the military in 1945. He served again as president from 1951 to 1954, when he committed suicide after being threatened with impeachment. This section on samba during the Vargas years draws on scholarship by Lisa Shaw (1999).

The Vargas government stressed industrialization and a work ethic that would support it, especially in Rio de Janeiro and São Paulo, supported new social welfare laws, and sought to promote a strong sense of national identity. His government used censorship to control the press and the entertainment industries, especially after 1937, and used the radio to broadcast nationalist messages and promote Brazilian music. Under the influence of censors, samba composers wrote fewer lyrics about *malandragem* and more about the work ethic promoted by the government.

In the years preceding WWII, the Vargas goverment was on good terms with Germany and Italy. The *Hora do Brasil*, the nightly radio program that featured government programming and Brazilian music, was broadcast in Germany and Italy in 1936. Once the war began, the United States made efforts to improve its relations with Brazil due to its strategic importance. The Good Neighbor Policy included cultural exchanges between the United States and Brazil, one result of which was the use of Brazilian songs in Disney animated features.

During the 1930s, a group of middle-class composers that included Noel Rosa (1910–1937), Ari Barroso (1903–1964), and Dorival Caymmi (b. 1914) made important contributions to the *samba-canção* repertory, which had been developed by composers for the musical theatre in Rio de Janeiro during the 1920s. *Samba-canção* (samba-song) emphasizes melody more than rhythm and has a more varied harmonic accompaniment compared to Carnaval sambas. *Samba-canção* was also known as mid-year samba because it was released outside of Carnaval season. Orlando Silva (1915–1978) was an important singer of *samba-cançao* on radio, in films, and on record, especially during the 1930s and 1940s. He recorded well-known sambas by Noel Rosa, including "Três Apitos" and "Feitiço da Vila."

One of the best-known sambas is Ari Barroso's "Aquarela do Brasil" (1939), an example of a substyle of samba called *samba-exaltação* for the way it exalts the Brazilian people, culture, and geography. Literally entitled "Watercolor of Brazil," and known in the English-speaking world simply as "Brazil," this song personifies Brazil as a "devious mulatto" and paints a nostalgic image of the old Northeast during the time of slavery. Prominently cited at the end of a list of idyllic descriptions is "meu Brasil brasileiro/Terra de samba e pandeiro" (my Brazilian Brazil/Land of samba and *pandeiro*). According to Shaw (1999), Barroso wrote this samba in order to celebrate a more wholesome image of Brazil than that found in other sambas and to praise the way of life found in Salvador, his favorite part of the country.

ACTIVITY 1.2 *"Aquarela do Brasil" is one of the most-recorded of Brazilian songs. The musical description that follows should apply to all but the most radically altered versions. Find a version in your library or online and follow along. A complete translation of the lyrics appears in Shaw (1999).*

"Aquarela do Brasil" is one of a handful of songs that are recognizable by their introductory accompaniment figure alone ("New York, New York" is another), a three-note figure that is played twice, once on the beat and once with syncopation. The first theme alternates long held notes on the exclamation "Ô," followed by quicker syncopated notes for the phrases that describe Brazil. Like most memorable standard songs, it takes this melodic and rhythmic idea and develops it, first in a major key, then in a minor one, and then in major again. Many readers will have encountered this song in Terry Gilliam's 1985 film *Brazil,* in which it symbolized a dreamworld for the protagonist, Sam Lowry, played by Jonathan Pryce.

Carmen Miranda Brings the Samba to Hollywood. The 1995 documentary by Helena Solberg, *Carmen Miranda: Bananas Is My Business,* narrates the recording and film star's life and career in the context of the Vargas era and the Good Neighbor policy. Most of the film consists of footage of Miranda performing and interviews with people who knew her. Solberg also includes her own reminiscences of Miranda and several brief fictional or dreamlike episodes.

Born in Portugal in 1909, Carmen Miranda emigrated to Rio de Janeiro with her family at a young age and grew up hearing samba. After being discovered while singing at a party at the National Institute of Music, she began a successful recording career with a repertoire of sambas and tangos, collaborated with the *sambista* Synval Silva, and began a long association with Aloysio de Oliveira and the group Bando da Lua, who accompanied her for many years. An invitation from impresario Lee Schubert to perform on Broadway in "The Streets of Paris" began her U.S. theatre and film career. Her colorful, fruit-laden costume was adapted from the traditional dress of *baianas* (Bahian women). The Solberg film includes excerpts of Miranda performing her best-known songs, including "Mamãe Eu Quero," "Tico-Tico no Fubá," "South American Way," and "O que é que a baiana tem?".

Miranda felt pressure to please two very different audiences: the international audiences who enjoyed her exoticism, and her Brazilian public, which perceived her to be adapting herself to a foreign stereotype of Brazil. She was hurt when a performance in Rio de Janeiro after her initial U.S. successes was greeted coldly. She replied with the song "Disseram que voltei americanizada" ("They said I came back Americanized"). She eventually became frustrated with the limited roles she was offered, and struggled to maintain a heavy performance schedule. She died in 1955 after collapsing during the filming of an American TV show, and was mourned by large crowds in Brazil (see Fig. 1.9). The composer Heitor Villa-Lobos is quoted in the film, saying "Brazil will always have an unpayable debt to Carmen Miranda."

CHORAM AMIGOS DA VELHA GUARDA

Ari Barroso, Josué de Barros, Assis Valente e «Russo do Pandeiro», profundamente comovidos, falam a O DIA sôbre a morte da maior intérprete da nossa música popular

MORREU

CARMEN MIRANDA

Depois do filme de televisão com Jimmy Durante o fim trágico no leito

O DIA

VIVEMOS EM MENTIRA DEMOCRÁTICA

UMA FACADA NO PEITO

FIGURE 1.9 *The front page of the Rio de Janeiro newspaper* O Dia *announces the death of Carmen Miranda.* *(Photo courtesy Contéudo Expresso, www.contentxp.com.)*

The singer and composer Caetano Veloso (b. 1942), in an essay in Perrone and Dunn (2001), recalls how young people of his generation were both proud of Carmen Miranda's achievements and ashamed of the image she projected. Later, she became a key reference for the *Trop-*

icália movement. Veloso's article praises her samba recordings of the 1930s and the precision of her gestures.

SAMBA AND CARNAVAL: THE SAMBADROME AND BEYOND

Carnaval in Brazil is a pre-Lenten celebration, a season of celebration that culminates in the three days preceding Ash Wednesday, the beginning of the Lent season that precedes Easter in the Christian liturgical calendar.

ACTIVITY 1.3 *Investigate a pre-Lenten Carnival in a location other than Brazil. Examples range widely, from New Orleans to Trinidad to Basel and Lucerne, Switzerland. Write a brief summary of what you learn, noting your sources carefully. If the time of year permits, attend a Carnival celebration in your area and share your experiences with the class.*

Carnaval was celebrated in Brazil well before the founding of the first samba school, Deixa Falar, in 1928. Carnaval developed from rowdy end-of-the-year celebrations that were practiced during the colonial era until the early nineteenth century, a prominent feature of which was throwing dirty water on people in the street from upstairs windows (a practice that continues in Carnaval in Olinda, near Recife). By the mid-nineteenth century, the polka was the preferred dance at Carnaval parties, where waltzes, schottisches, marchas, and mazurkas were also played (Tinhorão 1986: 112–13). By the early decades of the twentieth century, as the population of Rio de Janeiro grew and diversified, so did the participation in Carnaval. Groups from the middle and lower classes began parading together in costume, and rhythms for couple-dancing in ballrooms were replaced with those that were more appropriate for large processions, such as the marcha and eventually the samba (Tinhorão 1986: 121). Groups from Rio's *morros* (hillside slums) paraded in *blocos de sujos* ("ragamuffin bands," literally "groups of dirty ones" [Raphael 1990: 76]) and faced police repression when they went outside of their neighborhoods. The formation of the samba schools was an effort to legitimize the Carnaval groups formed by people who lived on the *morros*.

During the Vargas era the samba schools were given official recognition. In 1935, they were required to obtain licenses to parade and obliged to append the phrase *Grêmio Recreativo* (Recreation Society) to their names (Souza et al. 1988: 147); this is why the names of samba schools on the annual Carnaval compilation recordings (which began in 1968) are preceded by the initials "G.R.E.S.": Grêmio Recreativo Escola de Samba. In 1939, the government made it mandatory for the samba schools to use nationalistic themes for their parades (Souza et al. 1988: 149). Along with this official recognition came government subsidies for the samba schools, which were helping to make Carnaval into a major tourist attraction.

During their first decades, the samba schools were cooperative community organizations.

> The leadership and membership were entirely indigenous, coming from each individual neighborhood. Members gave from their own near-empty pockets to meet the schools' needs, and artisans gave freely of their skills to build the schools' floats. Female school members sewed costumes, men made their own instruments, the children caught the cats whose skins covered the homemade drums used in the rhythm section. Rehearsals for the Carnival parade were held in the dirt lanes of the *favelas;* when headquarters were built, local carpenters provided the labor (Raphael 1990: 77).

This is the seemingly idyllic time memorialized in the 1959 film *Orfeu Negro*, which has served as an introduction to Brazilian music and culture for generations of viewers. This film and several others on samba are discussed on the web site.

By the 1960s, the samba schools had increased greatly in size and had come under increasing pressures from outside their communities. Carnaval became more competitive, with lucrative prizes for the winning schools. In 1960, the Brazilian capital was shifted from Rio de Janeiro, which had served as the capital since 1763, to the newly constructed city of Brasília, which made tourism even more important to the economy of Rio de Janeiro. Samba schools came under the control of businesspeople from outside of their communities, some of whom were involved in illegal gambling. The schools' activities became more commercialized as more middle-class Rio residents became involved in their activities. Professional designers known as *carnavalescos* made carnaval parades and costumes ever more luxurious. The most prominent *carnavalesco*, Joãozinho Trinta, defended this practice in the 1970s with an often-quoted phrase: "pobre gosta de luxo; quem gosta da miséria é intelectual" ("poor people like luxury; it's intellectuals who like misery"; quoted in Souza et al. [1988: 154]). The location of the Carnaval parade shifted among various avenues in downtown Rio de Janeiro until the construction of the Passarela do Samba, known officially as the "Praça da Apoteose" (Plaza of Apotheosis, or "moment of crowning glory" in Charles Perrone's phrase [2001: 62]) and popularly as the Sambadrome in 1984.

The use of *enredos* drawn from Brazilian history and culture has continued to the present. Themes have included "The Second Marriage of Emperor Dom Pedro II," "The History of Rio's Carnaval," "Heroes of Liberty," "Brazil in the Year 2000," and, in 1988, celebrations of the centennial of the abolition of slavery in Brazil (Souza et al. 1988: 152–61). The 2004 compilation of *samba-enredo* includes tributes to the Amazon region, a public-service samba promoting the use of condoms, an appeal for traffic safety, a promotion of the use of alcohol for fuel, a samba in praise of science, and a tribute to the celebrity and children's TV show host Xuxa. *RGS* includes the *samba-enredo* "Nostradamus," performed by the GRC Escola de Samba Vai Vai from São Paulo.

The growth of the samba schools and of Carnaval in general coincided with the years of military dictatorship in Brazil (1964–1985). But as the authors of *Brasil Musical* point out, this should not be taken to signify support for the military governments on the part of samba composers or samba school participants. Since the return to democracy in 1985, the samba schools have continued to be the main focus of Carnaval and Rio de Janeiro's principal focus of tourism.

Carnaval is celebrated all over Brazil, and in each region, local traditions are included along with samba. Along with Carnaval in Recife, described above, Carnaval in Salvador is among the most important celebrations outside of Rio de Janeiro. As in Rio de Janeiro, Carnaval in Salvador in the nineteenth century included the more rowdy *entrudo* and an elite celebration that featured *marchas* (Moura 2001: 164–5). Due to its prominent role in the slave trade, Salvador historically has had a large Afro-Brazilian population, and has been an important center of the Afro-Brazilian religion *candomblé* (both descriptions still apply today). The Filhos de Gandhi (Sons of Gandhi) carnival group, known as an *afoxé*, was formed by a group of dock workers in 1949, inspired by Mahatma Gandhi's nonviolent struggle for Indian independence. In 1975, the first *bloco afro*, Ilê Aiyê, was formed. It drew on the symbolism of African movements for independence and was inspired musically by reggae and African-American artists such as James Brown (Moura 2001: 167; see also Crook 1993). Olodum, the most famous *bloco afro*, was formed in the 1980s. Olodum's samba-reggae songs included references to a wide range of African diasporic culture and became nationally and internationally popular, especially after the group's collaboration with Paul Simon, *Rhythm of the Saints* (1990). *Trios elétricos* are pop music bands who perform from atop enormous trucks carrying powerful sound systems. They began in the 1950s as an innovation of the duo Dodô and Osmar (Moura 2001: 168), and today they carry the top stars of *axé music*. This high-energy style, whose label combines a Yoruba word and an English one, adapts the samba-reggae, which is typically played by percussion ensembles, to a pop band format. Luiz Caldas, Daniela Mercury, and the band Chiclete com Banana are some of the best-known figures of *axé music*. Carlinhos Brown, the charismatic composer and performer from Salvador, leads several groups, including the percussion group Timbalada. His songs have been recorded by Caetano Veloso, Marisa Monte, Cássia Eller, Djavan, and the band Paralamas do Sucesso (Guerreiro 2000: 169), and he has toured and released recordings internationally.

In Salvador, as in Rio de Janeiro, Carnaval has been affected by tourism and the involvement of local elites, and this has tended to create spatial separations along the lines of socioeconomic class.

> Afro-Bahian music is now played on top of the *trio elétrico* trucks and is consumed by all. Meanwhile, the individual Afro-Bahian does not have access to the groups that play this music, for lack of sufficient material resources. Within two meters of each other are two distinct groups, attracting and repelling each other. On one side is the large, dark-skinned majority of the population of Salvador, anxious to occupy the spaces of Carnival. On the other is the light-skinned minority composed of local elite and middle-class revelers and the tourists from Brazil and abroad. It is not difficult to imagine how tense this unequal existence is and how such tension might be released. The largest Carnival groups employ between 400 and 800 security guards. On the other hand, everyone is there, close and far away, year after year (Moura 2001: 174).

In addition to the social separation, Moura finds that musical styles tend to occupy distinct spaces during Carnaval:

> On the main roads, *axé music* reigns, performed by the largest groups with the most popular artists who are admired and consumed by the

> general population. In the cross streets, alleys, parking lots, and public plazas, reggae, *pagode*, and *brega* [sentimental pop, discussed below] music is heard. The audiences of these two types of environments are not, however, completely fixed. The same person might pass several times, in the same day, between different musical areas and even between different worlds in the same city (2001: 174).

The music and musicians of Salvador and Bahia play a complex role in the story of samba and in Brazilian music in general. Musicians from Bahia were part of the musical culture that produced samba in Rio de Janeiro in the early twentieth century. Bahian composer Dorival Caymmi and his children are important figures in Brazilian popular music. Scenes of Bahian life inspired samba composers such as Ari Barroso. Guitarist and singer João Gilberto, one of the founders of *bossa nova*, is from Juazeiro, Bahia. Bahian artists Caetano Veloso, Maria Bethânia, Gilberto Gil, and Tom Zé were part of the *Tropicália* movement of the 1960s and have continued to produce important music ever since.

Most Brazilian musicians play or compose a samba at some point in their careers. As the authors of *Brasil Musical* put it, "In the country of samba, it's necessary to understand that each and every composer is a *sambista* at least once in his or her life" (Souza et al. 1988: 136). Among the composers and performers who have concentrated on samba are Cartola, Paulinho da Viola, Martinho da Vila, Jackson do Pandeiro, Elza Soares, Clementina de Jesus, Chico Buarque, Gal Costa, Nei Lopes, Leci Brandão, Beth Carvalho, Alcione, Clara Nunes, Zeca Pagodinho, and Jorge Aragão. *RGS* includes tracks by the well-known samba singers Leci Brandão, Elton Medeiros, Ivone Lara, Zizi Possi, Cartola, Nelson Sargento, Bezerra da Silva, Jards Macalé, and the Velha Guarda da Mangueira.

Recalling the interface metaphor from the preface, I urge readers to listen to as many of these artists as possible. A special favorite of mine is "Trem das Onze" (Eleven O'Clock Train), by Adoniran Barbosa, as performed by the vocal group Demônios da Garoa. The narrator has to cut short a romantic evening in order to catch the last train home and avoid causing his mother to worry about him. In terms of gender, the song dramatizes a conflict between male roles: the devoted lover vs. the dutiful son. But it is also a great song: a memorable melody, impassioned solo vocals and tightly blended vocal unisons and harmonies, and a skillful accompaniment.

The use of samba as a symbol of national identity has included sambas that directly address the strong influence of U.S. music and popular culture on Brazil. Two well-known examples are "Chiclete com Banana," by Gordurinha and Almira Castilho, first recorded in 1958, and "Eu Não Falo Gringo" by João Nogueira and Nei Lopes. The first song, recorded by Jackson do Pandeiro, the well-known singer of samba and *coco*, is a rich and multilayered creation. Musically, it blends samba with the instrumentation of Northeastern *forró* and chord changes that recall blues. The lyrics are a demand for cultural reciprocity between Brazil and the United States, represented in the lyrics as "Tio Sam" (Uncle Sam). "I'll only put bebop in my samba," the narrator sings, "when he [Uncle Sam] learns that samba isn't rumba." In return, "I want to see boogie-woogie with pandeiro and violão." Charles Perrone's introduction to *Brazilian Popular Music & Globalization* (Perrone and Dunn, eds. 2001) includes an extended discussion of this song. The second song, which dates from the 1980s, is a more pointed rejection of U.S. culture and influence, symbolized by the English language: "I don't speak gringo/I only speak Brazilian [. . .]. And the *pagode* was created there in Rio de Janeiro/My profession is *bicho* [the illegal lottery]/I sing samba the whole year long" (quoted in Galinsky 1996: 139).

Both songs are a reminder of a complex dynamic that has characterized Brazilian music—and, one could argue, all "American" musics in the hemispheric sense—throughout its existence. Brazilian musical genres such as the samba are blends of musical elements from within and outside of Brazil. Once the blend has attained a distinctive form and become a symbol of national identity and pride, as samba did in the 1930s, further blending is discouraged by those who consider themselves the guardians of tradition. This can be observed in the debate over whether *bossa nova* represents an outgrowth of samba or an influence of jazz, which will be addressed in the next chapter. Yet the process of cultural and musical blending is unstoppable, and a significant aspect of the creativity of Brazilian musicians has been the way they continuously renew established genres with elements of regional Brazilian musics and musics from abroad.

Pagode. The style of samba that has received the most attention in recent decades is known as *pagode*. It exists in two forms: a rootsy, backyard style of samba that flourished in the 1960s–1980s, and a more commercial style that dates from the 1990s to the present. The term *pagode* is the Portuguese equivalent of "pagoda," and has the general sense of a party, but the etymology is not mysterious. Folklorist Luís da Câmara Cascudo quotes an 1873 dictionary that linked the term, with a licentious connotation, to women who danced in Asian temples (1972: 659).

Ethnomusicologist Philip Galinsky traces the origins of *pagode* gatherings and the music played at them to the early twentieth century origins of samba itself, and links contemporary uses of the term to a movement in the 1960s and '70s that resisted the entry of middle-class people and business interests into *escolas de samba* and the resulting marginalization of the lower-income participants (1996). The Rio de Janeiro suburb of Ramos was a center of *pagode* activity, and it was there that the band Grupo Fundo de Quintal (The Backyard Group), viewed by many as the defining artists of rootsy *pagode,* was founded. Two members, Jorge Aragão and Almir Guineto, eventually became well-known solo artists. *Pagode* was distinguished by its instrumentation: to the cavaquinho, violão, and pandeiro, *pagode* muscians added four-string banjo; the *tan-tan* or *tantã,* a conga-like drum that rests on the player's lap and subsitutes for the *surdo;* and the *repique-de-mão,* a drum that is played with the hands. This group performed older sambas and added new ones with lyrics that chronicled daily life. Grupo Fundo de Quintal collaborated frequently with the noted singer Beth Carvalho. Another important *pagode* artist is Zeca Pagodinho, whose "Malandro é Malandró e Mané é Mané," a good example of *pagode* style, is included on *RGS.* In the late 1980s, *pagode* became nationally popular for several years before yielding to other popular music phenomena such as *sertaneja, lambada,* and *axé-music* from Bahia. As noted above, a more commercialized form of *pagode* emerged in the early 1990s, featuring romantic lyrics and an instrumentation that includes keyboards, drum set, and brass.

Pagode is distinguished musically by a slower tempo compared to *samba-enredo,* rich harmonies, and the use of the *partido-alto* rhythm and song form. Galinsky shows the *partido-alto* rhythm as follows:

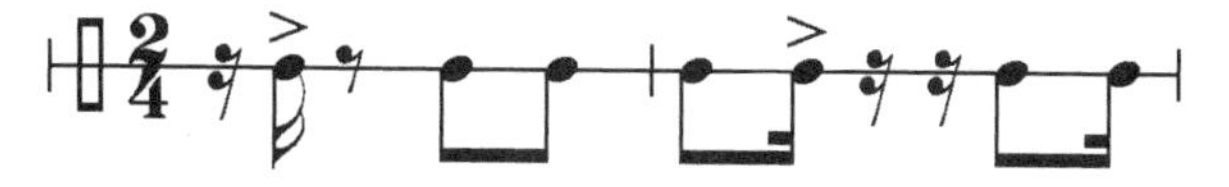

FIGURE 1.10 Partido-alto *rhythm.*

The typical *partido-alto* song form features a vocal duet, patterns of syncopated sixteenth notes that are tied across the beat, and the use of the harmonic cycle ii7–V7–I-VI7. It is one of a number of influences on *pagode.* Galinsky emphasizes that *pagode* originally referred to an informal party, and music played there and given the same label is an updated version of the sort of *samba de morro* that is played outside of the Carnaval season.

SAMBA TODAY: A RANGE OF MEANINGS

It is important to remember that there are many forms of samba. The semantic field of the term is very wide. The oldest uses of the term refer to any gathering of Afro-Brazilians that included music; the term *batuque* was also used in this way. Multiple styles of samba are practiced in northeastern states today, such as the *samba-de-roda* of Bahia. In Pernambuco, samba is used to refer to musical gatherings in general, often in a verb form (*sambar*, roughly analogous to "make music"). In the *maracatu* genre, the encounter of two master poet-singers is called a *sambada*. The term *pagode* also appears as a variant of the *coco*, a responsorial song form practiced in coastal northeastern Brazil. These styles and many more can be heard on *Música do Brasil*, the marvelous 4-CD collection of recent recordings of traditional musics by Beto Villares and Hermano Vianna (2000); it may be hard to locate in the United States, but it is well worth the effort.

What all forms of samba share is a role in creating a sense of national identity, a sense that they communicate something uniquely Brazilian, something rooted in Brazilian ways of making percussive music, of moving the body, and using language to comment on daily life in artful ways. Three recent recordings illustrate the range of its contemporary forms.

Samba Raro. *Samba Raro*, the 1999 CD by multi-instrumentalist Max de Castro, combines samples with newly recorded acoustic and electronic instruments and vocals in such genres as "samba jazzy," "afrosambabeat," "samba-lounge," "bossa-funk samba," and "drum 'n' bossa." Individual tracks pay tribute to established artists including Jorge Ben Jor, Baden Powell, Chico Buarque, Roberto and Erasmo Carlos, Geraldo Vandré, and Wilson Simonal, who also happens to be Max de Castro's father. The sound owes as much to soul, funk, rap, and electronica as it does to traditional samba. *Time* magazine singled out de Castro as an emerging talent in its "Music Goes Global" special issue, which at the time of this writing was still available on the Web. De Castro hopes that his music bridges the gap between markets as well as it does between styles. The *Time* profile quotes him as follows:

> De Castro has a goal in mind. "Most Brazilian musicians are labeled international artists," he says. "I will be very glad when I enter an

American record store and find *Samba Raro* not in the world-music section but beside people I admire like Prince and Stevie Wonder" (2001).

Eu Tiro é Onda. In 1998, the rapper Marcelo D2 of the group Planet Hemp released *Eu Tiro é Onda,* a mixture of samba with hip-hop and the product of a collaboration between Marcelo D2 and other Brazilian and U.S. rappers. Thematically, samba and hip-hop share a concern for narrating the reality of everyday life. Musically, samba's emphasis on the second beat of a slow duple meter lines up with the hip-hop's 2 and 4 backbeat, and layers of syncopated percussion are found in both. On "Samba de Primeira," samba rhythmic patterns and instruments such as *pandeiro* and *cuíca* provide the foundation for lyrics about life in Rio de Janeiro. The opening of "Batucada" features a women's chorus singing the samba "A Batucada dos Nossos Tantãs" (Sereno—Adilson Gavião—Robson Guimarães) in unison over a hip-hop beat. Marcelo D2's second solo CD, *À procura da batida perfeita* (2003), also explores the common ground between samba and hip-hop.

The Song "O Mistério do Samba." In 2000 the Recife-based band Mundo Livre S/A released the song "O Mistério do Samba" on the CD *Por Pouco.* The title is an allusion to Hermano Vianna's book of the same title. In a wry gesture apparently intended to counter the argument that there is a single samba essence, and to contest the commercialization of samba, the lyrics by lead singer Fred04 list all of the things that samba is not: *carioca* (from Rio de Janeiro), *baiano* (from Bahia), *africano* (African), *do salão* (of the drawing room), *da avenida* (of the avenue, or the Carnaval parade), *da cerveja* (about beer), *do Faustão* (associated with the popular TV host of that name). The list goes on. The music of Mundo Livre S/A is discussed further in Chapter 6.

ACTIVITY 1.4 *Collate the information about the history of Brazil presented in this chapter into a chronological outline. Continue to add to it as you study the book.*

This chapter has presented samba as a national music that exists in many varieties: *samba-enredo, samba de morro, samba-canção, pagode* (both kinds), *samba-de-roda,* and more. Its highly syncopated two-pulse beat animates colossal Carnaval parades, intimate backyard parties, and every setting in between. Samba lyrics offer insight into Brazilian nationalist sentiment, romantic relationships, gender roles, and political views. The history of samba follows the progress of Afro-Brazilians from traditional beginnings in the Northeast to migration to the large cities of the South, where samba was at first marginalized and later incorporated into the nationalist project of the Vargas years. Since then samba schools have grown and modernized along with the cities and the media that transmit the sights and sounds of Carnaval all over Brazil.

CHAPTER 2

Projecting Brazilian Identity Nationally and Internationally

CHORO: AN EARLY RIO DE JANEIRO INSTRUMENTAL STYLE

In Lapinha, a quiet, older Rio de Janeiro neighborhood, a group of musicians are gathered on a Saturday morning under shade trees in a small plaza. They are playing guitar, *cavaquinho*, *pandeiro*, clarinets, flutes, and soprano saxes. Over a rhythmic background of syncopated sixteeenth notes played on the *pandeiro*, the melodic instruments spin out long, graceful lines over rich and varied chord changes, with a melodic counterline in the guitar. This gathering is devoted to *choro*, a primarily instrumental genre that originated in the late 1800s. It's a called a *roda de choro*, literally a *choro* circle. *Rodas de choro* also happen in private homes (Figure 2.1).

Monday nights are devoted to *choro* at Bip-Bip, a tiny bar in the Copacabana section of Rio de Janeiro, a few hundred yards from the beach on a residential side street. Gathered around tiny tables, *choro* players play familiar tunes in a relaxed atmosphere. The proprietor, Alfredinho, reminds anyone who needs reminding that in order to avoid annoying the neighbors, any applause must take the form of snapping fingers.

In addition to these intimate settings, *choro* groups have appeared in concert halls throughout Brazil and abroad and in televised performances. Sound recordings of *choro* began in the 1920s.

Choro symbolizes Brazilianness because it is among the first distinctively Brazilian ways of composing and playing instrumental music. *Choro* compositions such as "Tico-Tico no Fubá" and "Brasileirinho" are among the most widely recognized pieces of Brazilian music. The story of *choro* intersects with that of samba: in the 1930s, samba percussion

FIGURE 2.1 *Henrique Cazes Quarteto. (L to R) Marcello Gonçalves, violão de 7 cordas; Omar Cavalheiro, contrabass; Beto Cazes, percussion; Henrique Cazes, cavaquinho.* *(Photo by Wilton Montenegro.)*

was added to the standard instrumentation of *cavaquinho*, two guitars and a solo instrument (typically flute), and sambas that adapted vocal lines to the instrumental *choro* melodic style were composed and recorded. A revival of interest in *choro* and other traditional Brazilian genres in the 1970s led to the emergence of a new generation of performers and composers, the acceptance of *choro* on equal terms with art music, the inclusion of *choro* in music education in Brazil, and the performance and appreciation of *choro* outside of Brazil. This section surveys these developments and includes close listening to a performance of "Língua de Preto" by the Henrique Cazes group.

The Emergence of Choro. Henrique Cazes, the *cavaquinho* player, composer, and author of an excellent study of *choro* (1998), starts his narrative of the genre in 1845, when the polka arrived in Rio de Janeiro, a time when social dances were shifting from group dances to couple dances. There are several explanations for the term "*choro*," which refers to weeping (literally it means "the act of weeping or crying"; the verb *chorar* means "to weep," "to mourn," "to lament"; *choro* musicians are called *chorões*). Cazes writes that the label comes from the melancholy way in which Brazilian musicians phrased polka melodies. The Brazilian music historian José Ramos Tinhorão links the term to the melancholy expression created by the modulations and low-register guitar counterlines that are characteristic of the genre (1986).

By the 1870s and 1880s, a group of composers and performers in Rio de Janeiro had begun to add *choros* to their repertoire of polkas, tangos, and *maxixes*, and pieces with the word "*choro*" in their titles began to appear. This group included the flutist Joaquim Antônio Callado (1848–1880), the pianists Chiquinha Gonzaga (1847–1935) and Ernesto Nazareth (1863–1934), and the clarinetist and saxophonist Anacleto de Medeiros (1866–1907). *Choros* from this period typically had three sections, with modulations between them, and used rondo form, in which the first theme returns in alternation with contrasting themes. The typical instrumentation was a flute, two guitars with six or often seven strings, and *cavaquinho*. Most of the performers were drawn from the urban lower-middle class and had civil service jobs that were compatible with spending large amounts of leisure time playing music. Before the jazz band instrumentation came into use in the 1920s, and while samba was still emerging, *choro* groups provided much of the music heard in cafés and private parties. Brass bands provided the music for public events on a larger scale, and many players received their musical training in bands. This included the ability to read music.

Northeastern Influences. Like the samba, *choro* incorporates elements of musical styles from Northeast Brazil. The guitarist and composer João Pernambuco (1883–1947) came to Rio de Janeiro from Pernambuco in 1902 and collaborated with the singer Catulo da Paixão Cearense (1866–1946), whose popularity was part of a vogue for Northeastern music. Pernambuco composed songs in the Northeastern genres of *coco* and *toada*, and solo pieces for guitar. His "Choro #2" may be heard on *RGS*. He was a member of the Grupo Caxangá and Os Oito Batutas along with Donga (an early samba musician) and the flutist, saxophonist, and composer Pixinguinha.

Pixinguinha. Pixinguinha and his group Os Oito Batutas were the first *choro* group to become nationally famous. They played for several months in Paris in 1922 and helped to raise awareness of Brazilian music at a time when other new American musics, such as jazz, were also growing in popularity in Europe. There was some opposition to their trip from people who did not want Brazil to be represented abroad by black musicians, and there was debate afterwards about the extent to which their music was influenced by jazz. Cazes suggests that the jazz influence may have been limited to the inclusion of the saxophone and the hybrid instruments banjo-*violão* and banjo-*cavaquinho*.

Pixinguinha's compositions form the core of the *choro* repertoire. Among his best-known works are "Carinhoso" (included on Yo-Yo Ma's 2003 CD *Obrigado Brazil* along with his "1 x 0 [Um a zero]"), "Ingênuo," "Segura Ele," and "Vou Vivendo." He was part of the historic 1926 meeting between samba musicians and intellectuals described in Chapter 1 and part of a musical circle that involved the cellist and composer Heitor Villa-Lobos, who played *violão* with *choro* groups. The recordings Pixinguinha's group made in 1928–1932 are significant because his arrangements blended the horns of the jazz band with Brazilian string and percussion instruments to create a distinctly Brazilian orchestral language (Cazes 1998: 71). It was around this time that samba percussion became a standard part of the *choro* group and lyrics were added to instrumental *choro* compositions. It was also the time that samba, with its more conversational lyrics and stronger rhythmic feel, became more popular than *choro*, which started to sound old-fashioned.

"Língua de Preto," the *choro* composition heard on CD track 1, was originally a polka. The recording presents it as performed in the current *choro* style. It was first recorded between 1907 and 1912 by the Banda da Força Policial do Estado de São Paulo, on the Odeon label. It was also recorded by the Banda da Casa Edison in 1913. Pixinguinha had success performing it as a teenager. Jacob do Bandolim recorded it on his first RCA release at a time when it was a practically forgotten composition; now it is a *choro* standard.

ACTIVITY 2.1 *As you listen to CD track 1, "Língua de Preto" by Honorino Lopes (1884–1909), performed by the Henrique Cazes group (see Fig. 2.1), count measures in a relaxed two beats per measure. This is how* choros *are notated in Brazilian editions. Listen for three themes and note when they occur using the CD's elapsed time. Note the similarities between "Língua de Preto" and works of early jazz, such as Ferdinand "Jelly*

Roll" Morton's "Black Bottom Stomp" or "Grandpa's Spells." Choro *and early jazz pieces both have multiple themes, syncopation, and breaks for solos.*

Jacob do Bandolim and Waldir Azevedo. In the late 1940s and 1950s, two highly gifted instrumentalists brought the *choro* back into national prominence. Jacob do Bandolim (1918–1969), a lifetime civil servant and master of the *bandolim* (a small string instrument with four double courses, similar to the mandolin), composed the very popular "Noites Cariocas," written with Hermínio Bello de Carvalho, and recorded new arrangements of obscure *choro* compositions. In 1964 he performed the solo part in a four-movement orchestral work dedicated to him, *Suite Retratos,* by Radamés Gnattali, which paid homage to four important figures in the history of *choro*: Pixinguinha, Ernesto Narareth, Anacleto de Medeiros, and Chiquinha Gonzaga. He also led the *choro* group Época de Ouro during the 1960s. The *cavaquinho* player Waldir Azevedo (1923–1980) had great commercial success with his compositions "Brasileirinho," an up-tempo virtuoso showpiece, "Pedacinhos do Céu," and "Delicado." According to Cazes, Azevedo is the *choro* musician who has had the most commercial success, because in addition to being an excellent instrumentalist, he composed tunes that were both extremely catchy and interesting from the point of view of instrumental performance. "Brasileirinho" can also be heard on Yo-Yo Ma's *Obrigado Brazil.*

The* Choro *Revival. The 1960s were a period of lower public interest in *choro,* during which a core group of players, including the composer Radamés Gnattali and the clarinetist and saxophonist Paulo Moura, continued to cultivate it in private *rodas de choro.* In the 1970s, there was a revival of interest in *choro* that has continued to the present among practitioners and fans of Brazilian instrumental music, with allowances for a brief vogue for jazz fusion in the 1980s. Ethnomusicologist Tamara Livingston dates the start of the *choro* revival to 1973, when prominent samba musician Paulinho da Viola, along with the critics Sérgio Cabral and Hermínio Bello de Carvalho, invited the group Época de Ouro to perform on the TV program *Sarau* (1999). Along with this program, Cazes cites the Northeastern group Os Novos Baianos, which combined rock with samba, *choro,* and *frevo,* and a general interest in things Brazilian that arose around this time to resist the ever-growing influence of U.S. cultural products (1998: 141). The *pagode* samba movement dates from this period. The venerable samba singer Cartola made his first solo recording in 1972, backed by a group that included *choro* musicians. "Quem me vê sorrindo" from this recording can be heard on *RGS*, and Cartola's "Alvorada" can be heard on the soundtrack of the 2002 Brazilian film *City of God*. *Choro* and samba share a similar rhythmic feel (though much lighter in the case of *choro*). The key difference between them is the primarily instrumental nature of *choro* and its emphasis on long, developmental melodic lines. The inclusion of *choro* among the genres that Brazilian musicians used to counter the influence of U.S. music shows that, like samba, *choro* symbolizes national identity.

Choro, *Art Music, and Jazz.* The composer Radamés Gnattali (1906–1988) was at the forefront of efforts to present *choro* on an equal basis with art music. He formed the Camerata Carioca, a chamber group active from 1979 to 1985, to perform *choros* and arrangements of classical works in concert programs that included *Tributo a Jacob do Bandolim, Vivaldi & Pixinguinha*, and *Uma Rosa para Pixinguinha*, and the LP *Tocar*. The composer Heitor Villa-Lobos modeled several works on the *choro* (see the section "Brazilian Art Music Briefly Surveyed").

Choro and jazz have shared characteristics for two reasons. First, they arose from similar conditions, as musicians in the United States and Brazil, many of them African-American or Afro-Brazilian, respectively, played European genres such as marches and polkas with more rhythmic energy and incorporated improvisation into their performances. In both genres, there was a productive interaction between musicians who learned music by ear and incorporated improvisation into their playing, and those who read music notation. Second, *choro* musicians have used elements of jazz style and instrumentation in their interpretations of *choro*. Severino Araújo (b. 1914), the saxophonist, clarinetist, and composer of *choros* such as "Espinha de Bacalhau," has used big band instrumentation to play *choro* with his Orquestra Tabajara for 60 years. Improvisation in traditional *choro* takes the form of melodic and rhythmic decorations of and variations on the themes, rather than the creation of new lines based on the harmony, as in jazz (though this does happen in the counterlines played by the seven-string guitar). Andrew Connell explores the relationship between *choro* and jazz in the context of a study of contemporary Brazilian instrumental music (2002).

Women in Choro. Playing *choro*, like much musical activity in Brazil, has traditionally been a male-dominated activity, but women have been involved since its earliest days, and women are prominent among contemporary players. Chiquinha Gonzaga, mentioned above, is noted in *choro* history as a composer and pianist, and her "Corta-Jaca" is a part of the *choro* repertoire. Research by Maurício Carrilho identified 123 women composers of *choro*, from Chiquinha Gonzaga to contemporary *cavaquinho* player Luciana Rabello, including Tia Amélia, Lina Pesce, and Carolina Cardoso de Meneses. Fourteen of them are represented on the CD *Mulheres no Choro* (Women in Choro, 2002; mp3 samples available at www.acari.com.br). And women are prominent among contemporary performers of *choro*, as noted in the following section.

Choro's *Current Vitality*. There are six signs of *choro*'s current vitality. First, a new generation of players and composers arose as a consequence of the 1970's revival, including *bandolim* players Joel Nascimento and Déo Rian; the virtuoso guitarist Raphael Rabello (1962–1995) and his sister, Luciana Rabello; and the saxophonists Mário Sève of the group Nó em Pingo d'Água and Daniela Spielmann of the group Rabo de Lagartixa. An even younger generation includes *cavaquinho* player Ana Rabello and *bandolim* player Bruno Rian. Second, opportunities to learn *choro* are increasingly plentiful. It is being taught in music schools, and method books, printed music, academic studies, and recordings are making the repertoire available to students. Third, *choro* is being performed at a high level by musicians outside of Brazil, including the Venezuelan *bandolim* player Cristóbal Sotto, the Japanese group *Choro* Club, the Japanese flutist Naomi Kumamoto, the U.S. mandolin player Mike Marshall, and the Egyptian *violão* player Ahmed El-Salamouny. Jazz at Lincoln Center in New York featured the music of Pixinguinha in a series of concerts in 2002 directed by Brazilian guitarist Romero Lubambo. Fourth, specialized record labels including Kuarup, Acari, and Biscoito Fino release *choro* recordings. Fifth, *choro* has a lively Internet presence in the form of informative and commercial sites. Finally, *choro* is present in the repertoire of Brazilian musicians who play other styles, including composer and multi-instrumentalist Hermeto Pascoal and accordionists Zé Calixto and Arlindo dos Oito Baixos (discussed in Chapter 4). *Choro*'s importance as a national music was reaffirmed in 2000, when then-President of Brazil Fernando Henrique Cardoso signed a decree that designates April 23, Pixinguinha's birthday, as the National Day of *Choro*.

BRAZILIAN ART MUSIC BRIEFLY SURVEYED

During the colonial period, 1500 to 1822, art music activity in Brazil was concentrated in religious institutions. Music was composed for church services, and musical instruction was part of the process of converting Amerindian groups to Christianity. In the second half of the eighteenth century, in conjunction with the prosperity provided by gold mining, musical life flourished in Minas Gerais (the state name means literally "General Mines"). When the Portuguese royal court moved to Rio de Janeiro in 1808, art music activity increased and European composers were attracted to the city (Béhague 2001).

With independence from Portugal in 1822 and the establishment of the First and Second Empires, (1822–1831 and 1840–1889, respectively), opera and chamber music were the most popular genres of art music. The most important of the opera composers of this period is Carlos Gomes, whose opera *Il Guarany* premiered at La Scala in Milan in 1870. Pianist and composer Louis Moreau Gottschalk (1829–1869) ended his brief but brilliant career in Rio de Janeiro, where he organized "monster concerts" involving as many as 650 performers.

In the late nineteenth and early twentieth centuries, musical nationalism led composers to seek inspiration in traditional music. The works of musicologist and author Mário de Andrade, discussed in Chapter 1, were influential during this period. The most significant of the nationalist composers is Heitor Villa-Lobos (1887–1959), whose works draw on traditional genres, especially *choro*. Among his best-known works are the *Bachianas Brasileiras*, a set of nine suites inspired by the music of J.S. Bach. Of these, the most frequently performed work is the "Aria-Cantilena" from the fifth suite, scored for soprano and cello (the composer's principal instrument).

During the remainder of the twentieth century, Brazilian composers kept pace with international trends in composition, including serialism, atonality, and neo-classicism. They did not, however, lose touch with Brazilian traditional and popular music. Radamés Gnattali collaborated with *choro* musicians; César Guerra Peixe made a study of *maracatu* in Recife; and Rogério Duprat was part of the *Tropicália* movement. Music for guitar has been a special area of interest on the part of Brazilian composers and performers, including guitarist Turíbio Santos.

BOSSA NOVA: THE INTIMATE SAMBA SOUND KNOWN WORLDWIDE

Bossa nova can be heard worldwide today in settings that range from a formal solo concert by guitarist and singer João Gilberto (b. 1931) to an informal gathering of friends who pass a guitar around and sing their favorite songs at the beach or in a sidewalk café. Most evenings in a jazz club or hotel lounge will include at least one *bossa nova* standard by Antonio Carlos Jobim (1927–1994) or a jazz standard performed with a *bossa nova* feel. *Bossa nova* is frequently used for TV, movie soundtracks, and background music. And for such a subtle style, home listening should be included in a list of ideal settings.

What draws listeners to *bossa nova*? Some of the appeal is intrinsically musical: *bossa nova* classics such as "Chega de Saudade," "Garôta de Ipanema," "Desafinado," "Corcovado," and "Insensatez" have beautiful melodies that are both tuneful and memorable, on the one hand, and extremely well crafted in terms of motivic development, on the other. The rhythm is interesting on several levels: the melodies use a syncopated rhythm that follows the accents of the Portuguese lyrics. The guitar accompaniment, originated by João Gilberto and known as *violão gago*, or stammering guitar, distills the samba's energetic percussiveness into a playful alternation between the strong beats and syncopated chords. The chord progressions are colorful and varied, with modulations to unexpected keys. The very sound of sung Brazilian Portuguese creates its own music.

Another part of the appeal is what *bossa nova* symbolizes: the beaches, nightclubs, and upscale apartments of Rio de Janeiro; the idyllic image of Rio de Janeiro that is shown in the film *Orfeu Negro*, a hopeful time of modernization in Brazil just before the 1964 military coup; the tropical setting of Brazil in general; and the sophistication of the late 1950s early 1960s. Rock'n'roll was around but had not come to dominate popular music, and mature listeners still listened to Frank Sinatra and Miles Davis, Stan Getz and Charlie Byrd. Both kinds of appeal, the musical and the symbolic, will be part of this discussion of *bossa nova*.

***The Term* Bossa Nova.** The term *bossa* existed as a Rio de Janeiro slang term before the musical style known as *bossa nova* emerged. According to ethnomusicologist Gerard Béhague, it meant "special ability, shrewdness, astuteness" (1973: 210). Tom Jobim explained the link between the word *bossa* and the sense of a knack or special ability:

> In Portuguese, a *bossa* means a 'boss'—a protuberance, a hump, a bump. . . . And the human brain has these protuberances—these bumps in the head. . . . So if a guy has a *bossa* for something, it is literally a bump in the brain—a talent for something. To say that he has a *bossa* for guitar would mean that he has a genius for guitar. So it has come to mean a *flair* for something—and *bossa nova* was a 'new flair.' (Quoted in Tesser 1989)

"Bossa" appeared in the lyrics to the samba "Coisas Nossas" (1932) by Noel Rosa, and in the 1940s the guitarist Garoto led a group called Clube da Bossa (Bossa Club) (Castro 2000: 150). Applied to the new style, *bossa nova* meant a new way of making music, the "new wave" or the "new thing." The first use of the term in this new sense was on a poster advertising a concert by Sylvia Telles, Carlos Lyra, Ronaldo Bôscoli, Roberto Menescal, and others at the University Hebrew Group of Brazil. The authorship of the poster copy is attributed to Moysés Fuks, the secretary of the group, who promised "a *bossa nova* evening." A few months later, it appeared in the lyrics of "Desafinado," by Tom Jobim and Newton Mendonça, as a reference to the new style that the song itself exemplified (Castro 2000: 150–53). These developments can be understood in a broader context as an expression of the modernizing trend that was energizing Brazil in the 1950s.

A **Bossa Nova** *Classic.* The essential elements of *bossa nova* were established by a core group of composers, lyricists, and performers in Rio de Janeiro in the late 1950s. The most prominent among them were Tom Jobim and João Gilberto. Jobim composed songs that form the core repertoire of *bossa nova*: he composed "Insensatez" (How Insensitive) and "Águas de Março" (March Rains); "Chega de Saudade" (No More Blues) and "Garôta de Ipanema" (The Girl from Ipanema), with Vinícius de Moraes, the poet and diplomat, and "Desafinado" (Out of Tune), "Meditação" (Meditation), and "Samba de Uma Nota Só" (One Note Samba) with pianist Newton Mendonça.

João Gilberto established the model for *bossa nova*'s guitar accompaniment and soft, rhythmically flexible singing style, starting with his 1958 recording of "Chega de Saudade." You can hear excerpts of this song, along with "Desafinado," "One Note Samba," "O Pato," and "Bolinha de Papel," on amazon.com. Unfortunately, the reissued CD from which the samples are taken has been out of print due to a dispute between Gilberto and EMI over alterations in the recordings and the fact that the tracks are presented out of order.

"The Girl from Ipanema."

ACTIVITY 2.2 *The classic version of "The Girl from Ipanema," recorded in March 1963 by Tom Jobim (piano), João Gilberto (voice and guitar), Stan Getz (tenor sax), Astrud*

Gilberto (voice), Tommy Williams (bass), and Milton Banana (drums), can be found on the Verve CD Getz/Gilberto *and the Verve/Polygram compilation* Bossa Nova Brasil. *For copyright reasons the lyrics are not reproduced here, but they are easily found in CD liner notes or on the Web in both Portuguese and English. Follow the suggestions for listening and then compare it to other kinds of samba, such as Carnaval samba.*

"The Girl from Ipanema" is a classic example of *bossa nova* style, a key aspect of which is the integration of the elements of the song in order to communicate a strong aesthetic effect. Voice, instrumental accompaniment, and lyrics are carefully coordinated so that no single element is more prominent than the others. This forms a contrast with the preceding style of singing *samba-canção,* in which a strong, theatrical voice projected over an orchestral accompaniment. Since this is the best-known song discussed in this book, and one of the most easily obtained, I have included more extensive suggestions for listening.

The song is 40 bars long in AABA form. Each A section is 8 bars long, and the B section is 16 bars long. In this recording, the musicians play the form four times. First the lyrics are sung in Portuguese; the second time the song is in English; Stan Getz plays the melody during the third chorus; and Tom Jobim's piano and Astrud Gilberto's English vocal share the fourth chorus.

00:00 The song begins with João Gilberto's wordless vocal accompanied by his guitar—in the key of D♭, not the key of F as in the published sheet music. The accompaniment includes bass notes on 1 and 3, played by the thumb, and chords softly plucked in a variety of rhythms (Figure 2.2):

According to guitarist Baden Powell, Gilberto derived the rhythm played by the thumb, which emphasizes the strong beats, from the *surdo*

FIGURE 2.2 *Three examples of guitar accompaniment rhythms in "The Girl from Ipanema."*

part in a samba percussion group; the rhythm of the syncopated chords, which are plucked by the fingers, is modeled on the more syncopated *tamborim* part (Reily 1996: 5).

00:08 Gilberto sings the first 8-bar A section alone. The melody begins on E♭, the 9th of D♭maj7, leaps down to the C, the major 7th, then steps to B♭, the 6th (see Chapter 4 of *Thinking Musically* for an explanation of intervals). Notice the slightly nasal tone of the vocal. This was something that set *bossa nova* apart from the then current style of singing, which was more full-voiced.

00:23 Williams (Bass) enters on the second 8-bar A section, followed by Jobim on piano. Gilberto sings softly, with a breathy tone. Compared to the sheet music, the rhythmic placement of his lyrics is sometimes ahead, sometimes behind.

The lyrics of the A sections describe a beautiful girl who passes by the narrator, evidently on her way to or from Ipanema, the beach in Rio de Janeiro's chic *Zona Sul* (southern district). The *e* in Ipanema is pronounced like the *ay* in *way*. The lyrics rhyme *graça* (grace) and *passa* (passes by); *dourado* (golden) and *balançado* (swaying movement); *mar* (ocean) and *passar* (pass by).

00:37 Gilberto begins the B section, or bridge, with a sustained sigh on "Ah!" The harmony has shifted up a half step from D♭ major to D major, and this melody note is the major seventh of the chord. Two more phrases begin with "Ah!", each one higher than the last. In bar 5 of the bridge, this "Ah!" is sung a minor 3rd higher, on the 9th of Dmi7; in bar 9, it's a minor second higher, on the 9th of E♭ mi7. In order to create rhythmic contrast with the A sections, the notes of the bridge melody are longer and less syncopated, and alternate between a sustained note followed by slow descending triplets.

The harmony of *bossa nova* compositions like this sounded fresh to U.S. jazz musicians because of the key relationships and root motions. Modulating up a half step for the bridge, however, is not unheard of in U.S. popular song. "Body and Soul," for example, modulates from the tonic D♭ major to D major at the start of the bridge. But U.S. popular songs typically modulate by means of short chord progressions, such as ii–V, that prepare the listener for the new key. In *bossa nova* compositions, the modulations are more typically direct, and the roots move by seconds and thirds rather than the fifths that are typical of U.S. popular songs. The bridge of "Garôta de Ipanema" modulates directly to the key a half step above the tonic key and then moves in root motions of fifths, thirds, and a tritone: Dmaj7, G7, Dmin7, B♭7♯11, E♭min7, B7 (the preceding chords last two measures each), Fmin7, B♭7♭9, E♭min7, A♭7♭5 (one measure each).

The lyrics of the bridge express the narrator's sadness and aloneness. The first phrase ends with the word *sozinho* (alone). The second and third phrases of the bridge rhyme: *triste* (sad) and *existe* (exists). The final phrase contains two rhyming subphrases ending on *minha* (mine) and *sozinha* (alone); the latter describes the aloneness of the girl who is passing by. (Remember to consult a full set of lyrics in order to put these words in context.)

01:07 Gilberto sings the final A section with a return to the syncopated melodies of the first two A sections. The lyrics describe how the world around the girl is made more beautiful by her presence, with rhymes on *passa* (passes) and *graça* (grace).

01:22 The second time through the song, Astrud Gilberto sings the English lyrics by Norman Gimbel. Each A section ends with the word "Ah," but the rhymes of the Portuguese lyrics are not preserved in the English ones.

01:51 On the bridge, the "Ah!" of the Portuguese lyrics has become "Oh," and instead of the two additional "Ah!"s of the Portuguese, she sings "How" and "Yes."

02:21 Astrud sings the final A section. Again the rhymes within the phrase are not preserved, but the "see" of the end of this section rhymes with "me" at the end of the bridge.

02:35 The third time through the song, Stan Getz plays an improvised solo that stays close to the melody and adds decorations to the ends of phrases. While Getz was not the first U.S. jazz musician to play *bossa nova,* he is the best known, and for good reason: his warm and breathy tone is the perfect instrumental counterpart to João Gilberto's voice, and his thorough harmonic knowledge enabled him to choose excellent notes to go with the chord progression.

03:38 The fourth time through the song, Jobim plays the melody on the piano in sparse, chordal phrases.

04:18 Astrud sings the bridge in English with fills by Getz.

04:48 Astrud sings the final A section with a counterline by Getz.

05:00 To end, Astrud repeats the final phrase as the chords repeat on D♭ M7 to D7♯11, with fills by Getz as the track fades.

"Garôta de Ipanema" is the most performed *bossa nova* composition and one of the most often performed songs of all time. It was first performed in 1962 as part of a nightclub show in Rio de Janeiro that featured Tom Jobim, Vinícius de Moraes, João Gilberto, and the vocal group Os Cariocas. Legend has it that Jobim and Moraes composed it while sitting in the Veloso Bar, which today is called Garôta de Ipanema; this is the version given by Reily (1996: 1). According to Castro (2000: 239), Jobim wrote the melody at home in Rio de Janeiro, and Moraes wrote the lyrics in Petrópolis, a small city outside Rio de Janeiro. A real girl did serve as their inspiration, however: Heloísa Eneida Menezes Paes Pinto, known as Helô, the daughter of a general, who was eighteen at the time. Jobim and Moraes did see her on the street. Her father and husband did their best to shield her from the publicity that the song generated. She is pictured, along with her daughter and Tom Jobim, in McGowan and Pessanha (1998: 69). Tom Jobim recorded the song for his album *The Composer of "Desafinado" Plays* (1963) a few months after recording it with Stan Getz. See the web site for suggestions for close listening to Jobim's "Desafinado" (Out of Tune) as performed by João Gilberto.

Other Ways of Playing Bossa Nova. Solo voice with guitar accompaniment, best exemplified in the solo performances and recordings of João Gilberto, has not been the only "authentic" way of playing bossa nova, even from the beginning. Vocals with large ensemble accompaniment, piano trios, and vocal groups are also important. Brazilian vocal recordings of the 1950s and 1960s often featured accompaniments by ensembles of brass and strings. João Gilberto's early LPs featured an accompanying ensemble that included strings. Jobim's *Wave* (1967), recorded in the United States in 1967, features the composer on piano, guitar, and harpsichord, along with bass, drums and percussion, flutes and piccolos, trombones, and a large string ensemble conducted by arranger Claus Ogerman, who also arranged and conducted the orchestra that accompanies the collaboration, *Francis Albert Sinatra & Antonio Carlos Jobim* (1967).

Piano trios (piano, bass, drums) with or without horns tend to play *bossa nova* with much more rhythmic intensity than do the groups that accompany vocalists. The trio with the most longevity was the Zimbo Trio, which was formed in 1964 by pianist Amílton Teixeira de Godoy, bassist Luiz Chaves Oliveira da Paz, and drummer Alberto Barsotti, and continued to perform with this lineup until 1999; the trio is still active. This group provided the accompaniment for an important TV show, "O Fino da Bossa," with vocalists Elis Regina and Jair Rodrigues, and has recorded extensively and performed all over the world. Other important trios are the Tamba Trio and the trio led by pianist João Donato.

One rhythm is prominent in the drum set parts of piano trio performances: in the first measure (counting in 2/4), 1, last sixteenth of 1, second eighth of 2; in the second measure, second eighth of 1, second sixteenth of 2. It is played on the rim of the snare with a stick while the drummer plays constant eighth notes with a brush in the other hand. This rhythm is sometimes referred to as a "*bossa nova clave*," by analogy with the Cuban clave rhythm. This is a misnomer, however, even though, as in clave, there are three accents in the first measure followed by two in the next. This rhythm is often played, but not with the consistency with which the clave is used to organize the parts of a Cuban musical ensemble. *Bossa nova* accompaniment is typically more varied and cannot be represented by a single rhythmic pattern.

Vocal groups were important in the radio, recording studio, and nightclub world of the 1950s out of which *bossa nova* emerged, and they remain a part of *bossa nova* performance style. *Bossa nova* composers were deeply interested in harmony, and carefully rehearsed vocal arrangements sounded their harmonies vividly. Along with Frank Sinatra and Sarah Vaughan, U.S. vocal ensembles such as Mel Tormé's Mel-Tones were avidly listened to and imitated by the young musicians who eventually formed the *bossa nova* scene. Os Cariocas is the vocal group associated most closely with *bossa nova*. The group was founded by Ismael Neto in 1942, and had already established itself through recordings and performances when it recorded "Chega de Saudade" with accompaniment by João Gilberto in 1958. Another important *bossa nova* vocal group is the Quarteto em Cy, formed originally by four sisters from Bahia named Cyva, Cynara, Cybele, and Cylene. Tom Jobim's later concerts and recordings typically included a female vocal ensemble as part of his Banda Nova.

ACTIVITY 2.3 *To summarize what you have learned thus far about the musical characteristics of* bossa nova, *make a compilation organized by categories such as the song form, melody, harmony, accompaniment, vocal style, or any other you consider appropriate. Then, do an online search for recordings by these vocal groups. Use any one song you can find to listen for the traits you just listed. Write an analytical statement about what you hear, or construct your own listening guide with timings.*

Bossa Nova *and Jazz.* Jazz was an important part of the musical tastes and repertoires of the principal figures of *bossa nova*. Stan Kenton was very popular among the *bossa nova* crowd due to his interest in Latin American music and the sophisticated harmonies created by his arrangers. Julie London's *Julie is her name* (1958), on which London's soft vocal is accompanied by Barney Kessel on guitar and Ray Leatherwood on bass, had a strong impact on *bossa nova* musicians. On songs like "Cry Me a River," the minimal accompaniment allows every nuance of London's vocal to be heard. According to Castro, guitarist Roberto Menescal "spent hours listening to the record 'Julie Is Her Name'" (2000: 84). Brazilian musicians absorbed jazz style through movies and live performances. U.S. artists including Lena Horne, Sarah Vaughan, and Nat Cole performed at the Copacabana Palace hotel in Rio de Janeiro, where they could both pass on jazz style to their Brazilian fans and learn about Brazilian music. For further discussion of *bossa nova*, jazz, and art music, see the website.

The Sound of a Modernizing Brazil. *Bossa nova* emerged during a hopeful time in Brazilian history. President Juscelino Kubitschek, in office from 1956 to 1961, put the country on a modernizing course that also included the construction of a new national capital city, Brasília, and the construction of a network of highways and accompanying growth in the production of cars and trucks. Continuing a trend of nationalist development that had begun during the Vargas era, he created the slogan "fifty years [of development] in five." The population of the major cities grew rapidly during this time as Brazil became more industrialized. Millions of workers from the Northeast migrated to Rio de Janeiro, São Paulo, and Brasília. Brazil won the World Cup in 1958, 1962, and 1970, which made soccer star Pelé world-famous. Brazilian filmmakers of the Cinema Novo movement, including Carlos Diegues, Glauber Rocha, and Nelson Pereira dos Santos, made important films that explored life in the *favela* (urban shantytown) and the *sertão* (backlands). Brazilian novelists were prominent in the so-called boom in Latin American literature. Jorge Amado's novel *Gabriela, Clove and Cinnamon* was a bestseller. Academic interest in Brazil and Latin America in general increased greatly during the 1960s. The works of Brazilian scholars such as Gilberto Freyre received close attention, especially from scholars who were interested in understanding why race relations in the United States and Brazil, which share so many similarities, turned out so differently.

Tom Jobim linked the *bossa nova* movement directly to this modernizing trend. In an interview just before he left for the 1962 Carnegie Hall *bossa nova* concert, he stated

> We are not going to sell [Brazil's] exotic side, of coffee and carnival. We are not going to wheel out the typical themes of underdevelopment. We are going to pass from the agricultural to the industrial era. We are going to use our popular music with the conviction that it does not only have its own character, but also a high technical level. (Tinhorão 1986: 242; quoted in and translated by Reily 1996: 6)

Prior to *bossa nova*, most listeners abroad associated Brazilian music with the exotic figure of Carmen Miranda, who brought sambas to Hollywood along with her brightly colored and fruit-laden costumes. Caetano Veloso's appreciation of Miranda notes that for young listeners in the 1950s, her music was a source of both pride and shame:

> In 1957, the recordings she made before she came to the United States in 1939 sounded archaic to our ears, and those she made in the United States seemed ridiculous: "Chica chica bom chic," "Cuanto le gusta," and "South American Way" were the opposite of our craving for good taste and national identity. (2001: 39)

Later in the same article, Veloso finds much to praise in Miranda's recordings, and notes the echo of her that he heard in "The Girl from Ipanema":

> When *bossa nova* burst on the scene in the United States—in other words, the world—we felt that Brazil had finally exported a highly refined quality product. But the fact that the style had been inaugurated by a single off the *Getz/Gilberto* album—"The Girl from Ipanema" sung beautifully in English by Astrud Gilberto—creates the impression of a cool-jazz Carmen Miranda. Not only does Astrud's voice spring like a luscious fruit from Tom Jobim's dense harmonies, the character praised in the song, the girl from Ipanema, seems to be wearing fruit on her head [a reference to the costumes Miranda wore in Hollywood musicals]. (2001: 42)

While it represented modernity, *bossa nova* also represented the worldview of a relatively privileged and homogeneous group of young people in Rio de Janeiro. Its focus on "o amor, o sorriso e a flor" (sun, smiles, and flowers), the title of João Gilberto's second album, and on themes of sea and sun, as expressed in the Ronaldo Bôscoli and Roberto

Menescal song "O Barquinho" (The Little Boat), eventually became grounds for criticism by those who wanted popular songs to express the more difficult reality of the lives of the majority of Brazil's population.

There were efforts by members of the *bossa nova* movement to broaden its range of themes and musical styles. Poet Vinícius de Moraes collaborated with guitarist and composer Baden Powell (named after the founder of the Boy Scout movement; his full name is Baden Powell de Aquino) to compose songs on Afro-Brazilian themes, such as "Berimbau," which recalls the sound of the instrument used in *capoeira* (see Chapter 3). Guitarist and singer Carlos Lyra and singer Nara Leão collaborated with old-guard samba musicians including Cartola, Nelson Cavaquinho, and Zé Keti. And Edu Lobo's song "Chegança" introduced Northeast Brazil's musical gestures, such as the raised 4th scale degree, into *bossa nova*.

TROPICÁLIA: CULTURAL CANNIBALISM, LATE '60s STYLE

Lasting roughly from 1967 to 1969, *tropicália*, or *tropicalismo*, was a popular culture movement animated by the spirit of artistic "cannibalism," a phrase from a 1928 manifesto by Oswald de Andrade. The lasting significance of *Tropicália* is that it showed how Brazilian popular musicians could absorb the most diverse international cultural elements, especially rock, combine them with elements of Brazilian culture, especially from Bahia, the home state of many of the participants, and form them into something distinctively Brazilian. The popular music branch of *Tropicália* included Caetano Veloso, Gilberto Gil, Tom Zé, Gal Costa, Nara Leão, the conductor and arranger Rogério Duprat, and the rock group Os Mutantes (Rita Lee, Arnaldo Baptista, and Sérgio Dias). The term *Tropicália* was borrowed from the title of an art installation by Hélio Oiticica.

Caetano Veloso and Gilberto Gil are the two most prominent figures associated with *Tropicália*. They came to national prominence through their participation in televised song contests after moving from their native Bahia to São Paulo in 1965 and provoked controversy at the 1968 festival, which had prohibited the use of electric guitars, by playing them anyway. Veloso composed the song "Tropicália" in 1967, with lyrics that combine traditional and modern images to form an imaginary landscape of Brazil in a time of great change. Gil, like the *tropicalistas* as a group, was very interested in the music of the Beatles, and his

1967 song "Domingo no Parque" (Sunday in the Park), which describes an encounter between two *capoeira*-playing friends whose encounter in the park turns into a violent episode fueled by jealousy, was modeled on "A Day in the Life." The musical arrangement is inspired by the music of *capoeira*, which is described in Chapter 3.

Vocalist Nara Leão, who had been active in the socially engaged branch of *bossa nova*, recorded "Lindonéia," by Caetano Veloso, on the 1968 LP *Tropicália, ou panis et circensis*, the movement's key recording. A *bolero* with string accompaniment, the song combines fragmented descriptions of a girl named Lindonéia with jarring images of violence ("dead dogs in the street"). It was inspired by a painting by a Rio de Janeiro artist that parodied Da Vinci's *Mona Lisa* (Sanches 2000: 62). Combining diverse lyrical images and sounds, including recorded noise manipulated in the recording studio, is typical of the songs produced by *Tropicália* artists.

Vocalist Gal Costa recorded "Não Identificado" (Unidentified) and "Baby," both by Caetano Veloso, who joined her on vocals on the latter. Both songs make reference to the music of pop icon Roberto Carlos, who was in his rock'n'roll phase at the time, in both their lyrics and their arrangements. The high degree of craft with which the arrangements are done and the inclusion of electronic noise add a layer of complexity and irony that is not found in Carlos's style. Costa went on to become one of the most important vocalists of Brazilian popular music, performing and recording songs by all of the country's important songwriters, including Tom Jobim, Ari Barroso, Dorival Caymmi, Chico Buarque, and Carlinhos Brown.

One of the most experimental members of the *Tropicália* circle was—and continues to be—Tom Zé, also from Bahia. His compositions combine elaborate arrangements for conventional instruments with the sounds of machines. His song "Parque Industrial" (Industrial Park), which was also included on the 1968 *Tropicália* LP, drips with irony as it describes a Brazil in which "industrial progress/will bring our redemption." Zé continues to produce highly original music and to attract new listeners. One of my Brazilian musician friends likes Zé's CD *Fabrication Defect* (1998) so much that he has a full-size, full-color tattoo of the cover art on his arm.

Tropicália effectively ended in 1969, when Caetano Veloso and Gilberto Gil were arrested by the military government and then spent several years in exile in London. The music and the ideals of the movement, however, have remained influential, inspiring both musicians and authors. Veloso and Gil released *Tropicália 2* in 1994 to commemorate the movement's twenty-fifth anniversary. Dunn's academic study in English (2001) and Sanches's journalistic account in Portuguese (2000) document the movement, its conceptual basis, and its counterparts in other artistic media. The CD *Tropicália Essentials* (1999) collects all of the songs mentioned here and more, with lyrics in Portuguese and English and informative liner notes by Marcelo Fróes and Ricardo Pessanha.

MPB: SOPHISTICATED SONGWRITING WITH A POLITICAL EDGE

The term *MPB* (*música popular brasileira*) came into use in the 1960s to designate popular music of high artistic achievement that drew from Brazilian musical traditions and used acoustic instruments. It was intended to distinguish its practitioners' music from rock, but since then *MPB* artists have incorporated a wide range of styles, including rock. According to Charles Perrone, author of the first book-length study of *MPB* in English, which devotes chapters to Chico Buarque, Caetano Veloso, Gilberto Gil, Milton Nascimento, and João Bosco and Aldir Blanc,

> MPB is now frequently used to refer to the music of artists who made their marks in the late sixties; the acronym also differentiates the work of those songwriters from the production of the eighties' generation, which is clearly dominated by the rock sound (1989: x).

Songs by *MPB* artists have carefully crafted lyrics, the aesthetic impact of which is only partially understandable by non-Portuguese speakers, since the effects often depend on the interplay between sound and meaning. While they may draw on well-known traditional genres, *MPB* artists typically transform their models and present them in unique arrangements. Martha Ulhôa de Carvalho, in a study of the music of Milton Nascimento, Chico Buarque, and Roberto Carlos, notes that

> In terms of composition, one of MPB's basic structural constraints is the interaction of content and form. Each MPB tune is a unique piece, both in the originality of the lyrics and the appropriateness of the music to that poetry (1990: 331).

MPB songs are open to multiple levels of interpretation, especially those composed in the 1960s as disguised protests against the military government. This quality is highly prized by the core audience for *MPB*, which, according to Carvalho, consists primarily of the generation of the country's cultural elite that came of age in the 1960s, and found in the music of Chico Buarque, especially, an articulation of its political aspirations. As a sign of how Brazil has changed, Gilberto Gil is currently the national Minister of Culture in the government of President Luiz Inácio "Lula" da Silva.

One such veiled protest song is Chico Buarque's samba "Apesar de Você" (In Spite of You, 1971). Ostensibly directed toward an ex-lover, the song is a direct critique of the military government that looks forward to the day when it will be gone. Another is "Cálice" (Chalice, 1973), written with Gilberto Gil, which draws a parallel between the biblical text "Father, take away this cup from me" (Mark 14:36) and "the despair of a subject who has been silenced by an implied repressive authority" (Perrone 1989: 32). The parallel depends on the similar sound of *cálice* (chalice) and *cale-se* (shut up!). Perrone relates the dramatic story of its censorship during a live performance: as police removed one microphone from the stage, Buarque moved to another, until he was finally silenced. "Thus, before a large audience, government agents dramatically enacted the song's central message" (1989: 34).The song remained censored until 1978. It can be heard on David Byrne's compilation, *Brazil Classics 1: Beleza Tropical.* Readers are urged to consult Perrone for explications and translations of many of Buarque's songs and to listen to the original recordings.

One of the most distinctive sounds of *MPB* is the soaring voice of Milton Nascimento, whose music, according to Carvalho, became a symbol of national identity during the transition to democracy in the mid-1980s. By that time Nascimento was already established as one of the principal figures of *MPB*. The recordings *Clube da Esquina* (Corner Club) and *Clube da Esquina 2* (1972 and 1978, respectively) brought him to national prominence along with a group of collaborators from his home state, Minas Gerais, that included Márcio Borges, Fernando Brant, Ronaldo Bastos, Lô Borges, Beto Guedes, and Toninho Horta. He has also collaborated with Wagner Tiso, Eumir Deodato, Wayne Shorter, and Gilberto Gil.

Nascimento's music exemplifies the way in which *MPB* artists draw on regional music to create a sound that speaks to a wide audience. Minas Gerais has a long tradition of religious music, which can be heard in Nascimento's preference for slower melodies with long phrases, the rhythm of which is derived more from the speech rhythms than from a regular pulse. His wordless vocals resemble the *aboio* (cattle call), and his accompaniments often include *viola* (double-coursed steel-string guitar). Nascimento's falsetto tones are said to remind listeners of the sound of an oxcart, a high-pitched rasp emitted by the friction of wheel and axle (Carvalho 1990: 332–3). The song Carvalho uses to exemplify these traits is "Canção da América" (Song of America), which he composed with Fernando Brant.

Carvalho asks why, given its regional associations and the class position of its principal audience, Nascimento's music became a national symbol:

> Although Nascimento's style addresses Brazilians in general, it speaks particularly to a specific social class, conveying aspects of the ethics and aesthetics of the so-called intellectual middle class and élite. Nevertheless, in the early 1980s politicians supporting the campaign for a direct vote for the presidency used Nascimento's music as a symbol of Brazilian identity. At that time his style, however élitist, appealed to all the Brazilians who wanted a change from the suffocating military dictatorship (1990: 322).

She finds that his music was effective in the context of political rallies not so much because of the political content of the lyrics—songs by Chico Buarque are much more pointed in this respect—but because of the power of his voice to move people's emotions. This also helps him attract listeners who may not speak Portuguese. I have heard him sing in Radio City Music Hall in New York and in concert with Gilberto Gil in Recife, and in both places the audience responded to him with affection.

MÚSICA BREGA: SENTIMENTAL SONGS LOVED BY MILLIONS

Just as samba music drives the celebration of Carnaval, and *bossa nova* expresses the modernizing sophistication of the 1950s–1960s, *música brega* taps into the taste of Brazilian listeners for songs that express strong sentiments in direct, unpretentious ways. This music has a huge audience throughout Brazil and in other Latin American countries, but it is either unknown to most North American listeners of Brazilian music or it is dismissed as just another example of the international romantic pop ballad, just as *música sertaneja*, might be dismissed for its resemblance to U.S. country music (discussed in Chapter 5). To ignore this music would be to neglect an important aspect of the musical experiences of millions of Brazilians.

Música brega is the sort of music heard on AM radio stations that define their audiences as working-class and, probably to a lesser extent, middle-class. (The Brazilian public is strictly categorized by IBOPE, the national opinion research firm, into classes A through E on the basis of their purchasing power and possessions.) The term *brega,* which means "tacky" or "tasteless" and is typically contrasted with *chique* (from the French *chic*) or stylish, came into widespread use in the mid-1980s (Araújo 1988: 50). *Música brega* is what one might hear in taxicabs or on jukeboxes in working-class bars. It is played by amateur vocalists who accompany themselves on MIDI keyboards and by bands whose name starts with *Banda* (band) or solo acts whose name ends with *e seus teclados* (and his or her keyboards). It is performed in the largest live venues in the country and in TV specials, and recorded on millions of records, tapes, and CDs.

The Romantic Balladry of Roberto Carlos. Roberto Carlos is the most artistically accomplished artist of the romantic ballad genre, which can be grouped as part of *música brega.* Carlos began his musical career by playing in rock'n'roll bands and singing *samba-canção* and *bossa nova.* His first LP featured a cover of "Splish Splash," Bobby Darin's 1958 hit. He achieved national fame as part of the *Jovem Guarda* (Young Guard, in contrast to the Old Guard of samba composers), a group that included Erasmo Carlos (no relation), who became his long-time songwriting partner, and the female vocalist Wanderléia. The *Jovem Guarda* TV show ran for four years in the late 1960s and became extremely popular among young people, inspiring new slang terms and fashions. *Jovem Guarda* is by no means a forgotten fad. A 5-CD compilation released in the mid-1990s sold well among teenagers, and hits by *Jovem Guarda* bands are routinely covered by contemporary groups (Gilman 1996).

Though most of the songs Roberto Carlos recorded during this period were escapist fare that would be labeled "teenybopper" in the United States, some more hard-edged material was included, such as "Quero que vá tudo pro inferno" (Everything Can Go to Hell), which, according to Gilman, "had been a reply to the more nationalistic critics and musicians who didn't accept any pop mixture that defiled the 'purity' of Brazilian music" (1996).

In the words of one Brazilian critic, "Rock learned to speak Portuguese with Roberto Carlos" (Ferreira dos Santos, n.d.), and it did so in terms that spoke clearly to the everyday concerns of ordinary Brazilians. Like Elvis Presley, Carlos also made films.

In the late 1960s, Carlos's repertoire shifted toward the romantic ballad and songs that express Christian devotion. In 1970 he recorded "Detalhes" (Details), written with Erasmo Carlos, which is considered "one of the most beautiful romantic songs in Brazilian popular music" (Ferreira dos Santos, n.d.). By the early 1970s he was already Brazil's top-selling musical artist. In 1974 he broadcast the first of what has become an annual series of Christmastime TV specials, now a national tradition on TV Globo, the nation's largest network. As Brazil's modernization continued in the 1960s and 1970s, more people could afford TV sets; the influence of television and especially of TV Globo has been heavily studied by social scientists.

> "For Brazilians, Roberto Carlos is as much a part of Christmas as a turkey is for you" in the United States, said Jotabe Medeiros, a pop music critic for the daily *O Estado de São Paulo*. "For a lot of people, their first musical memory is getting a Roberto Carlos record as a Christmas present" (Rohter 2003).

By the late 1970s his annual releases were selling more than one million copies, and a tour in 1978 reached audiences totaling more than 250,000.

Carlos began touring internationally in the late 1970s and released a record in English in 1981; he has also sung in Spanish, including the CD *Canciones Que Amo* (1997), and Italian ("Canzone Per Te," 1988). In 1982 he received an award from CBS records for selling more than 5 million records outside his native country. In 1984 and 1985 his songs were being played more than 3,000 times daily on radio in Brazil. He won a Grammy as best Latin American singer in 1988. In 1994 he became the first Latin American to sell more records than the Beatles: 70 million copies; his sales now total 100 million. In 1998 his third wife, Maria Rita, was diagnosed with cancer, and Carlos slowed his recording and broadcasting activity in order to be with her until her death the same year. He returned to performing in 2000 after a year of mourning. He left Sony (formerly CBS), his longtime label, and recorded an "Unplugged" special for MTV in 2002. He dedicated his 2003 CD, *Para Sempre* (Forever), to his late wife.

Roberto Carlos is unironically called the "King of Brazilian popular music," and he has a huge following of devoted fans.

> For [Caetano] Veloso, Roberto Carlos, as he is universally known here, represents a "profound Brazil" whose appeal is so vast that he is immune to trends and tastemakers. "He could with good reason be called the Elvis of Brazil," Mr. Veloso wrote in "Tropical Truth," his recently published autobiography. "He has been called the King, a title that he sports even today, without anyone denying it to him" (Rohter 2003).

He reaches these fans by singing songs that address the concerns of ordinary people in simple, direct language. How direct? In "Sua Estupidez" (Your Stupidity), he sings, "Your stupidity won't let you see that I love you." In addition to songs about romantic love or religious devotion ("Quando Eu Quero Falar Com Deus" [When I Want to Talk with God]), his songs tell stories from the lives of taxi drivers ("O Taxista") and truck drivers ("Caminhoneiro," a cover of John Hartford's "Gentle On My Mind"—think of Glen Campbell's version—with new lyrics in Portuguese). He has courted his female audience by recording songs in praise of women who are short, or overweight, or 40 years old, or who wear glasses. His live performances mix new material with hits from his whole career, and he is content to keep performing his fans' favorites. Carlos is intensely private and usually limits his interviews to one press conference in December when his yearly album is released. He stated in 2003, "I don't like to put songs in the show that the audience doesn't know yet" (quoted in Ferreira dos Santos, n.d.). He traditionally gives flowers to people in the first rows of his concerts. His songs have been recorded by many other Brazilian artists, including the singers Marisa Monte and Maria Bethânia. His musical style is similar to that of Julio Iglesias, yet he is much less known in the United States. Suggestions for listening to "Detalhes" (Details), one of Carlos's favorite songs, are found on the web site.

Like most singers of his generation, Roberto Carlos was strongly influenced by João Gilberto. While Carlos's vocal delivery is more intense and emotional, with occasional cracks in his voice at especially sincere moments, his rhythmic phrasing has some of Gilberto's conversational independence from the beat. This is not music that invites listeners to sit back and be impressed. The repetitiveness of the melody invites listeners to sing along.

Roberto Carlos *is* the "King" of Brazilian popular music because his songs allow listeners to feel their emotions more intensely. They strike some of the same emotional chords as *telenovelas* (prime-time TV dramas) do. Roberto Carlos has kept his fans listening and buying records and concert tickets for decades. This is no small achievement. Okky de Oliveira explains the key to his success this way in an essay on Carlos's official web site:

> . . . this man was born with a special gift: no one knows the soul of his people better than he does. In his youth, he was the leader and guide of his generation. In his maturity, he became the best chronicler of our enormous, inexhaustible vocation to fall in love, and to live love in all its romantic fullness.

Not surprisingly, there is a Brazilian feature film dedicated to Roberto Carlos, with songs by him (including "Detalhes") included in the action as well as on the soundtrack. *O Caminho das Nuvens* (The Middle of the World, 2003), directed by Vicente Amorim, tells the story of a father who leads his family on a journey of nearly 2,000 miles by bicycle, from Paraíba in the Northeast to Rio de Janeiro, in search of a job that will pay 1,000 *reais* (approximately $300) per month. His wife and son sing songs by Roberto Carlos at restaurants in exchange for handouts, and the children sing them as they ride. The film gives a realistic portrait of small town life in the Northeast, including a stop in Juazeiro do Norte, Ceará, at the shrine of Padre Cícero, a priest who became the object of popular devotion after his death in 1934.

The national musics discussed in Part I form a complex portrait of Brazil and Brazilians. Several themes tie them together. Songwriters express affection for the country itself, its landscape, and its people. The population shift from rural to urban in the early to mid-twentieth century is reflected in the growth of samba from a marginal music in Rio de Janeiro into a national symbol. Recording and broadcast media, beginning with records and radio early in the twentieth century and continuing with TV and films, have helped musicians attract national audiences. Composers and lyricists have demonstrated a high degree of verbal artistry in their crafting of lyrics. The Brazilian government, especially during the Vargas period and the 1964–1985 dictatorship, used cultural policy to control musical expression. These national musics thus enabled Brazil to enter the global musical market. In the course of the twentieth century, Brazil's musical image changed from that of a provider of exotic music to one of ultra-sophistication.

CHAPTER 3

Expressing Afro-Brazilian and Indigenous Identity

CAPOEIRA: MUSIC, MOVEMENT, AND THE LEGACY OF ZUMBI

A visitor to an outdoor market in Salvador, capital of Bahia state in Brazil's Northeast, is likely to encounter a pair of dancers in the center of a ring formed by musicians, fellow players, and onlookers, who trade whirling kicks, evade them with graceful cartwheels and headstands, including moves reminiscent of break-dancing, and occasionally trip each other or knock each other to the ground with well-timed head butts. They do this to the accompaniment of one or more musical bows, *pandeiro*, scraper, and drum, along with solo songs and choral responses. This is *capoeira*. *Capoeira* can be described as a game or martial art with music, as a form of dance with vocal and instrumental accompaniment, as a drama, and as a philosophy and worldview that emphasizes liberation and embodies reciprocity. J. Lowell Lewis, echoing anthropologist Clifford Geertz's term, calls it a "blurred genre" (1992: 1) because it straddles the boundaries of dance, music, and sport.

Capoeira is played or performed at regular practices and special ceremonies at academies (*capoeira* schools); in contests and tournaments; in public places including markets, plazas, parks, and beaches; and in folklore performances. It is always played by a pair of players. In a street performance, all of the dancers or players are likely to be men and boys, but women also learn *capoeira* and study at *capoeira* academies in Brazil and around the world. The players wear T-shirts (often white) and long white pants or warm-up pants, and either wear tennis shoes or go barefoot. Figure 3.1 shows a pair of *capoeira* players at an indoor performance.

A sequence of *capoeira* play is structured by a three-part musical form: the *ladainha* (literally "litany") is a solo song by the *mestre*, or leader of

FIGURE 3.1 *Mestre Cobra Mansa (foreground) and a student play capoeira at the opening of Cobra's academy in Washington, D.C.* *(Photo by Greg Downey, from his book* Learning Capoeira *[2005: 5]. Used by permission.)*

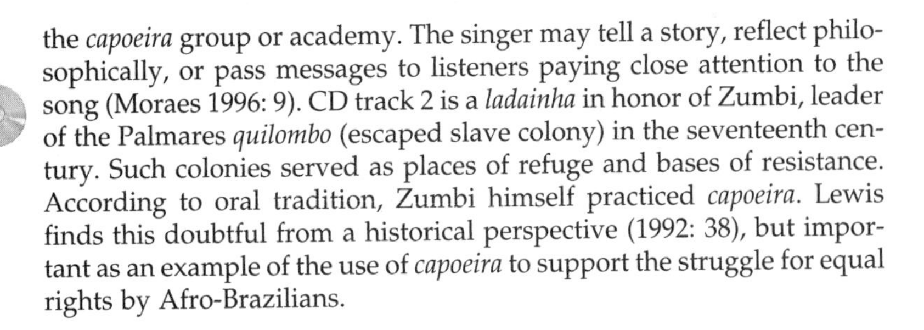

the *capoeira* group or academy. The singer may tell a story, reflect philosophically, or pass messages to listeners paying close attention to the song (Moraes 1996: 9). CD track 2 is a *ladainha* in honor of Zumbi, leader of the Palmares *quilombo* (escaped slave colony) in the seventeenth century. Such colonies served as places of refuge and bases of resistance. According to oral tradition, Zumbi himself practiced *capoeira*. Lewis finds this doubtful from a historical perspective (1992: 38), but important as an example of the use of *capoeira* to support the struggle for equal rights by Afro-Brazilians.

ACTIVITY 3.1 *As you listen to CD track 2, "Ladainha: Rei Zumbi dos Palmares" and follow the text and translation (cited from SFCD 40465 notes, p. 24), pay close attention to the way the* berimbaus, pandeiros, atabaque (cylindrical drum), reco-reco, *and* agogô *enter and establish the Angola pattern (a partial transcription is provided in Figure 3.2). Fol-*

low Mestre Moraes's singing of the ladainha, *and discuss the lyrics. Write a brief statement on how the lyrics connect the historical moments of Zumbi's time and the abolition of slavery with the present.*

A história nos engana	History deceives us
Diz tudo pelo contrário	Says everything contrary
Até diz a abolição	Even says that abolition
Aconteceu no més de maio	Happened in the month of May
A prova dessa mentira	The proof of this lie
É que da miséria eu não saio	Is that from misery I do not escape
Viva 20 de novembro	Long live the 20th of November
Momento pra se lembrar	Moment to be remembered
Não vejo em 13 de maio	I don't see in the 13th of May
Nada pra comemorar	Anything to commemorate
Muitos tempos se passaram	A long time passes
E o negro sempre a lutar	And the black man will always struggle
Zumbi é nosso herói	Zumbi is our hero
Zumbi é nosso herói, colega velho	Zumbi is our hero, old friend
Do Palmares foi senhor	Of Palmares he was the leader
Pela causa do homem Negro	For the cause of the black man
Foi ele quem mais lutou	It was he who fought the most
Apesar de toda luta, colega velho	In spite of all the fighting, my friend
O Negro não se libertou, camarada!	The black man did not liberate himself, comrade!

The second part, CD track 3, a *chula,* includes solo singing with choral refrains. During the *ladainha* and the *chula,* the players crouch near the *mestre* and wait to enter the *roda,* or playing circle.

ACTIVITY 3.2 *Follow the leader/chorus singing of the* chula *and* corrido, *which follow directly after the* ladainha. *(Text cited from SFCD 40465, notes p. 24, translation by the author.)*

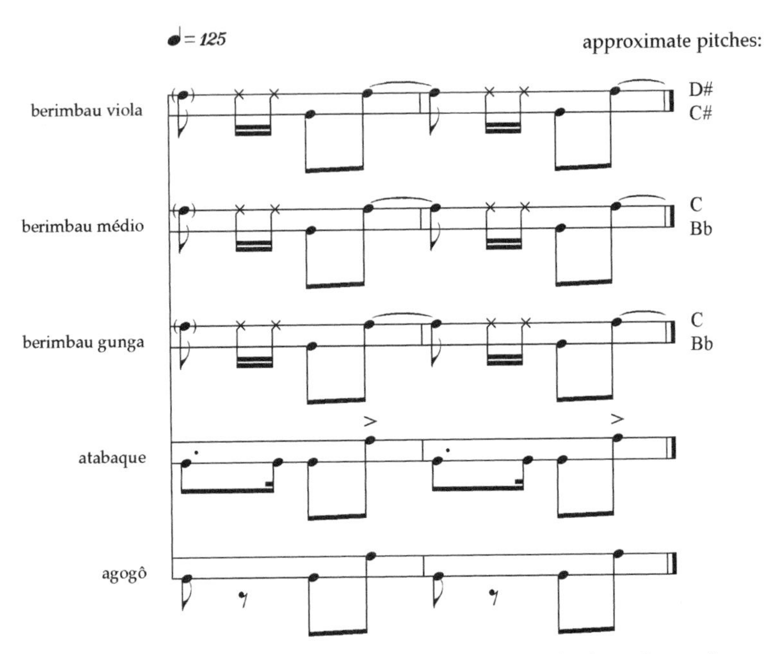

FIGURE 3.2 *Percussion parts for "Ladainha: Rei Zumbi dos Palmares."*

Iê, É hora é hora (leader)/Iê, É hora é hora, camará (chorus)
(Iê is a characteristic exclamation used in *capoeira.*)

	It's time, It's time/It's time, it's time, my friend
Iê, vamos embora/Iê, vamos embora, camará	Let's go
Pela barra afora/Iê, pela barra afora, camará	Beyond the bar [sandbar, perhaps]
Iê, Viva meu Deus/Iê, Viva meu Deus, camará	Praise God
Iê, viva meu mestre/Iê viva meu mestre, camará	Praise my teacher
Iê, quem me ensinou/Iê, quem me ensinou, camará	Who taught me

The third part of the musical form is made up of *corridos,* sequences of choral refrains. During this part, with more continuous singing, the players enter the *roda* for their stylized combat, which usually lasts around two minutes. CD track 4 is a *corrido* that refers to Saint Barbara, who is honored along with Iansá in the Afro-Brazilian religious pantheon. (Text and translation cited from SFCD 40465 notes, pp. 24–5.)

O Santa Bárbara que relampuê, O Santa Bárbara que relampuá
Santa Barbara will [bring] lightning

Because *capoeira* is practiced in many cities outside of Brazil, it may be possible to take or observe a lesson yourself.

ACTIVITY 3.3 *If there is a* capoeira *academy near you, visit a class. Make an oral presentation to the class on what you learned there.*

The movements of *capoeira* take place within a strict constraint: only the hands, feet, and head are supposed to touch the ground. The principal movements include the *rasteira,* a low sweeping kick; headstands (as shown in Figure 3.1); the *cabeçada,* or head butt, typically applied when an opponent is doing a headstand; the *aú,* or cartwheel (*fechado,* with knees bent); a money grab, used to pick up money contributed by onlookers; and many others. One *capoeira* master's attempt to codify the moves resulted in a table of nearly 40 movements (Lewis 1992: 222–3). These movements occur against the background of the *ginga,* the basic flowing, rocking step that connects them.

***The* Orquestra *and the* Berimbau.** The instrumental music of *capoeira* is performed by an *orquestra,* the players of which are expected to know the song repertoire and instrumental techniques as well as the movement repertoire (Figure 3.3). The most distinctive sound, without which there can be no *capoeira,* is that of the *berimbau,* a musical bow of African origin. The player holds the bow in the left hand, which also holds a large coin that is pressed against the string to change its pitch. An open, hollow gourd is attached to the lower end of the *berimbau,* and players use it to change the pitch and timbre of the instrument. The single steel string is taken from a car tire. The player's right hand holds a thin wooden beater and a small basket rattle, the unpitched sound of which combines with the pitched tones of the stretched wire.

FIGURE 3.3 *Boca do Rio (Marcelo Conceição dos Santos, left) and Cizinho (Tarcisio Sales Trinidade) play capoeira in Salvador.* *(Photo by Greg Downey, from his book* Learning Capoeira *[2005: 142]. Used by permission)*

Three *berimbaus* are typically present in the *capoeira* instrumental group. The lowest-pitched, called *berimbau gunga* or simply *gunga*, plays in the lowest register and plays the principal rhythmic pattern. The *berimbau médio* plays a rhythm that complements that of the *gunga*. The highest-pitched, called *berimbau viola*, plays variations on the basic rhythm. The rest of the instrumental group is made up of one or more *pandeiros* (large tambourines), one *agogô* (double metal bell), *reco-reco* (notched bamboo scraper), and an *atabaque* (tall single-headed drum). Figure 3.3 shows the *capoeira* instrumental group.

The *berimbau gunga* plays a melodic-rhythmic pattern, called a *toque*, which sets the pace for the movement of the players. The *toque* is formed from three tones: the tone produced by the open string, a higher tone produced by pressing against the string with a large coin (typically a whole step higher than the fundamental tone), and a buzzing tone produced by dampening the string's vibrations with the coin. The principal *toques* include Angola, São Bento Grande, São Bento Pequeno, Iúna, Santa Maria, Cavalaria, and Jogo de Dentro. They are demonstrated on the first of two CDs by the Grupo de Capoeira Angola Pelourinho (GCAP) on the Smithsonian/Folkways label (1996).

ACTIVITY 3.4 *As you listen to CD track 5, the Angola* toque, *focus your attention on the sound of the* berimbau. *The* berimbau *produces a rich blend of pitched, harmonic sounds (sounds whose vibrations follow the ratios of the overtone series) and percussive sounds without identifiable pitch.*

Capoeira players depend on the *berimbau* accompaniment for specific *toques*, for the tempo of play, and for specific phrases that suggest the timing for movements in the game (Downey 2002: 501–3). During the long period of apprenticeship, players learn to integrate their movements with the sound and rhythms of the *berimbau* using what could be described as full-body hearing. Players use the groove established by the *berimbau* to choose unexpected moments in which to launch an attack on their opponent. "*Capoeiristas* described to me the experience of 'listening for' the right moment to attack in the overlapping rhythms of an orchestra's overlapping *berimbaus*" (Downey 2002: 501).

Capoeira: *Other American Martial Arts and the African Heritage.* According to Lewis (1992), *capoeira* is one of a number of martial arts in the Americas that have grown from African roots. These include *l'agya* in Martinique, *maní* in Cuba, *kalinda* from Trinidad, and "knocking and kicking" in the southern United States, Brazil was a major destination of the Atlantic slave trade, and slavery continued there until 1888, longer than in any other country in the western hemisphere. The trade was fueled by the demand for labor on the sugar plantations of Brazil's Northeast, the region that includes Salvador, and later by the coffee plantations in South Brazil, most notably São Paulo state (see Figure 1.1).

The Grupo de Capoeira Angola Pelourinho, which is heard on this book's CD, traces its lineage of teachers to Africa: Mestre Benedito (*mestre* is a title that indicates respect for a master performer and teacher) came from Angola, and taught Mestre Pastinha (Vicente Ferreira Pastinha, 1898–1981), who taught João Grande (João Oliveira dos Santos, born around 1933), who taught Mestre Moraes, who created the GCAP (Moraes 1996: 4). In writing about this, and while he respects the importance of this lineage, Lewis describes *capoeira* as a Brazilian transformation of musical and movement practices that were widespread in central, west, and southern Africa (1996: 25–6). For example, the *berimbau* is very similar to the musical bow used by the Shona and San peoples, and Bantu and Yoruba terms appear in songs and as instrument names.

Capoeira: ***Resistance and Revolt.*** The conditions of Brazilian slavery and resistance to it are responsible for the specific character of that transformation. In order to survive, slaves cultivated *malícia,* or cunning, which enabled them to disguise resistance as innocuous play. This quality is prized in *capoeira* today. Resistance also took the more overt form of slave revolts and the founding of *quilombos*, or runaway slave communities. The most famous of these is Palmares, which existed for much of the seventeenth century. *Capoeira* oral tradition portrays Zumbi, the last king of Palmares, as a *capoeira* master, though Lewis argues that the game reached something like its present form much later, in the late eighteenth century, when large urban populations of Afro-Brazilians existed, and especially after 1889, when the Brazilian republic was founded (1992: 38, 42). What is significant about the association of *capoeira* with Zumbi and the *quilombo* of Palmares is the spirit of rebellion, resistance, and liberation that its present practitioners are able to draw from it.

One common story has it that *capoeira* was a martial art developed by slaves to aid in rebellions and escapes, but that it had to be disguised as a dance to fool the masters, who had forbidden all martial training to slaves. *Capoeira* players agree that even after abolition, a *capoeirista* would never carry a gun, or even use one captured in a fight. It was a matter of pride that one did not need a firearm to emerge victorious (Lewis 1992: 40–1). Today this spirit is directed toward socially engaged projects intended to improve the lives of Brazilians of African heritage, and the legacy of slavery is echoed in the names of *capoeira* groups, such as the well-known Grupo Senzala (the word *senzala* refers to slave quarters) in Rio de Janeiro.

Capoeira Regional ***and*** **Atual.** There are two other substyles of *capoeira,* besides that of *Angola,* which thus far has been the focus of this section. *Capoeira Regional* was developed by Mestre Bimba, who founded an academy in 1927 for the teaching of *capoeira* in a formal setting as a martial art. Bimba's academy was recognized by the government ten years later. In 1953 Brazilian President Getúlio Vargas called it "the only truly national sport," and in 1972 it was recognized as a national sport by the Brazilian Boxing Federation (Lewis 1992: 60–1). Bimba introduced a more formal approach to the teaching of the sport, with graded levels of accomplishment, and attracted middle- and upper-class Brazilians to the sport. *Capoeira Regional* tends to emphasize martial arts–style self-defense, while *Angola* is more improvisatory. A recent synthesis of the two styles, called *Capoeira Atual* (or up-to-date), is associated with

Mestre Nô in Salvador. Barbara Browning, a scholar and practitioner of *capoeira*, samba, and *candomblé*, puts the issue of *capoeira* styles into perspective by stressing the importance of individual creativity: "While some people will tell you there are two basic styles of *capoeira*, there are in fact as many as there are great *capoeiristas*" (1995: 89).

The practice of *capoeira* has spread around the world in recent decades, due in large part to Brazilian teachers including Jelon Vieira, the first master to begin giving regular lessons in the United States, and Bira Almeida, known as Mestre Acordeon. *Capoeira* has been shown in feature films, including *Only the Strong* (1993). It is regularly celebrated in newspaper articles as a fitness trend, and *capoeira* centers are found all over the world.

MUSIC OF BRAZIL'S INDIGENOUS PEOPLES

In his concise and engaging overview of music and dance in the tropical forest region of South America, anthropologist Anthony Seeger imagines two moments in which an imaginary observer hovers above the forest and listens (1998). In the first moment, before outsiders entered the region in large numbers, one would hear the sounds of flutes, reed instruments, solo and group singing, chanting, shouts, rattles, stamping feet; one would see rituals enacted by elaborately costumed and painted dancers, grouped by sex and age, or a shaman using music for healing. In the second moment, after decades of logging, burning, mining, road-building, and migration of outsiders, recorded music from outside the region predominates, and indigenous ritual music and dance must compete with it for the attention of the young people. Indigenous music has become endangered, just as plants, animals, and habitats have. This section describes the ritual use of music by the Kayapó-Kikrin. As in other indigenous groups, music and dance function together to ensure the reproduction of the society and to bridge the gap between human and natural worlds.

MUSIC OF THE KAYAPÓ-KIKRIN: A RITUAL OF AN AMAZONIAN PEOPLE

The Kayapó are an indigenous Brazilian people who live between the Tocantins and Xingu Rivers in Pará, in the Amazon region of northern Brazil (Figure 3.4). According to anthropologist Terence Turner, who has worked extensively with this group,

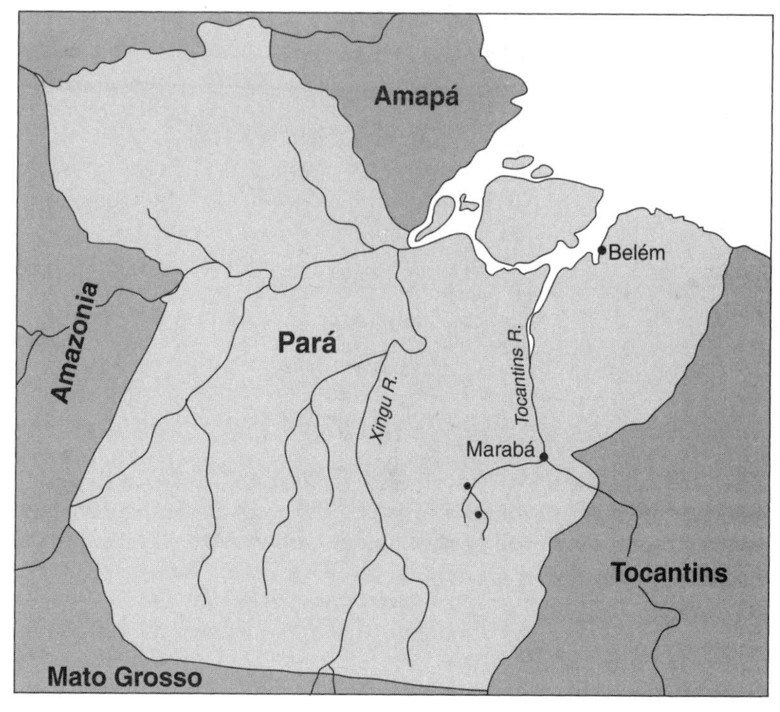

FIGURE 3.4 *The Amazon Region.*

The Kayapo have been in direct, if often intermittent and violent, contact with Brazilian society for about 150 years. Their society has undergone important changes in that time. First as a raiding society increasingly dependent upon plunder from Brazilian settlements, and more recently as owners of valuable gold mines and stands of mahogany from which they have extracted a sizable income over the last decade, the Kayapo are no strangers to commodities and money (1995: 148).

ACTIVITY 3.5 *Find this region on a map of Brazil. To acquaint yourself with the Amazon territory of North Brazil, and particularly Pará within it, find reliable print and Internet sources of information and write a brief essay summarizing what you learn, such as the size of the region and its size relative to the rest of Brazil, the population of the area, who the groups are, and where the population centers are.*

I will illustrate this section on the peoples of this area by an excerpt from the Smithsonian/Folkways CD *Ritual Music of the Kayapó-Xikrin.* I am indebted to the work of Lux Boelitz Vidal and Isabelle Vidal Giannini, who wrote the extensive liner notes (from which you can learn much more about what I introduce here), and to Max Peter Baumann and Linda K. Fujie, who made the recordings and photographs, respectively.

The Xikrin of the Cateté River, the Kayapó subgroup whose music I will discuss, live on forested land near the Tocantins River. The other subgroup lives near the Xingu River. They reside on lands that the government has designated as theirs, but they face constant encroachment by outsiders. Whereas in the popular imagination the Amazonian peoples may be thought to have always lived in their region of the forest, the present-day Kayapó communities share a history of many years of migration, and the forming of new subgroups. The Xikrin of the Cateté River settled there between 1930 and 1940. There was a further split in the 1960s over the issue of how to interact with outsiders, followed by a reconciliation. Since then their numbers have grown. They engage in hunting, fishing, gathering of forest products, and agriculture. While their material culture is relatively simple, their ceremonies and associated bodily decorations are elaborate.

In the decades preceding the 1980s, the Kayapó had not practiced some of their ceremonies because their population had dwindled. Since the 1980s, as the population grew and their way of life was being strongly threatened, they resumed the cycle of ceremonies.

The recording included on CD track 6 comes from a 1988 female naming ritual, *nhiok,* in which 15 girls received their name (Figure 3.5). The *nhiok* in turn is part of a set of initiation rituals that take place over five years; it was preceded by a hunt by the mature men and a male naming ritual. To begin the *nhiok,* the mothers of the girls who are to be initiated prepare a meal and paint their daughters' faces and bodies. The fathers prepare feathered headdresses and belts. A group of men begin singing the *nhiok* chant and dancing while the name-recipients are still in their houses. Then the name-recipients come out of their houses and

FIGURE 3.5 *Kayapó girl during* nhiok *ritual, August 1988. (Photo by Linda Fujie. Used by permission.)*

stand with their arms extended and their hands behind their necks, a position that is associated with the hummingbird, as are other parts of the ritual. They are accompanied by their female name-givers and formal friends. Next a group of men perform dance that moves out from the central plaza, stops in front of each name-recipient, and circles around her, her name-givers, and her friends. This part is known as the hummingbird's dance because it resembles the characteristic motions of the hummingbird in flight. The hummingbird is significant because its feathers are burnt and used to make a remedy that serves as protection against jaguars.

The next part of the ritual is a dance performed by a men's society that is associated with the jaguar, which their body painting is intended to resemble. Now the girls receive their names along with feathered belts, slings, and headdresses. The next day, two helmets with feathered decorations, representing the jaguars, and an eagle claw are constructed. After a ceremonial meal and the conclusion of the male naming ritual, two men who represent jaguars are adorned with feathered headdresses. The jaguars receive a food offering from the father of each of the girls being initiated. At sunset the girls being initiated form a group and sit with their backs to the setting sun while the jaguar men, now transformed into eagles, accompanied by a larger group of men, sing the Harpy eagle's chant, *okkaikrikti*, which is heard on CD track 6. This goes on all night, ending with the painting of the fathers of the male and female initiates.

ACTIVITY 3.6 *As you listen to CD track 6, "Okkaikrikti," note the imitation of the eagle's call, which can be heard twice at the opening of the track and twice more at 1:16. While the Kayapó use a bamboo trumpet, gourd rattle, and transverse flute in other musical activities, this chant is sung unaccompanied. The text is translated by Vidal and Giannini as follows:*

The claws of the harpy eagle will claw the nhiok [females being initiated]
Breathe and come through the path
Breathe and keep seeing hummingbird feathers being born

Try your hand at making a transcription of the melody of this chant. Then analyze the melody to answer questions such as these: How many phrases are there? Do you hear melodic repetition? How many different pitches do you hear? Are there fluctuations in tempo? Mark stressed pitches so that you can think about the rhythm: Is it pulsating rhythm? If so, did you hear groups of pulses in a regular organization, or is the rhythm less regular than that? How would you describe the vocal quality?

The Kayapó and the Environment. The Kayapó naming ritual discussed above is part of a system of social reproduction that is adapting to changing conditions. In an article that focuses on the Kayapó of the Xingu region, Terence Turner explains how such rituals are related to the ways in which the Kayapó make use of the Amazon forest for their subsistence, and thus to their political relationships with Brazilian society and the environmentalist movement (1999).

The Kayapó have been portrayed in the anthropological literature both as natural environmentalists and as exploiters of the forest for material gain, but Turner (1999) argues that the Kayapó are neither. Their traditional means of deriving subsistence from the forest, including slash-and-burn agriculture, hunting, and fishing, developed over centuries during which natural resources seemed limitless. As logging, mining, and road and dam building have put pressure on their way of life, they have adapted to changing conditions by skillfully combining traditional rituals with political activism.

The Kayapó have become one of the best-known Amazonian Indian groups due to their political environmental activity. One of their leaders, Ropni (also called Raoni) collaborated with Sting to raise awareness of threats to the Kayapó way of life from logging and mining companies. After some Kayapó leaders became corrupted by the profits from collaborating with Brazilian mining companies, the younger generation of leaders rejected the mining agreements. In 1989, the Kayapó organized a protest at Altamira against a dam on the Xingú River that attracted worldwide attention (see map, Figure 3.4). Kayapó leaders timed the 1989 Altamira demonstration to coincide with the end of the New Corn Ceremony, and called on the Kayapó subgroups to attend in complete family groups (for a photo, see Verswijver 1992: 25). The ceremony celebrates the myth of the origin of corn in a forest tree, and as part of the ritual a tree is cut down. The Kayapó support sustainable uses of the forest (and have even allowed limited commercial logging on their lands), but showed strong opposition to the dam project, which would have destroyed the capacity of their lands to sustain their lifestyle. Continuing to fight for their cause, Kayapó leaders participated in Earth Summit in Rio de Janeiro in 1992, and expelled gold miners from their territory in 1994 because of the environmental damage and health problems caused by the mining. Turner explains how Kayapó culture is not a rigid recipe for action, but a flexible system that adapts to changing conditions.

Inspired by Indigenous Music. Composer, guitarist, and singer Marlui Miranda, a Brazilian Indian, has been creating works inspired by the music of various Amazonian indigenous groups for more than two decades. Her best-known CD is *Ihu—todos os sons* (Ihu—All of the Sounds, 1996), on which she interprets music of numerous indigenous groups, including the Kayapó. Her collaborators on this CD include Gilberto Gil and Grupo Uakti. On other projects she has collaborated with Egberto Gismonti and Milton Nascimento. Her compositions are based on research in indigenous communities, and she has worked with anthropologists and indigenous rights groups and lectured in Brazil and internationally. She composed music for and performed on the sountrack of the 1991 Hector Babenco film *At Play in the Fields of the Lord.* Her work has been recognized by numerous awards and grants.

Composer, pianist, and guitarist Egberto Gismonti's sojourn in the Xingu region of the Amazon basin with the Yualapeti Indian tribe and his relationship with Yualapeti shaman, Sapain, is well documented musically in compositions such as "Yualapeti" and "Sapain" and in the recordings *Danças das Cabeças* (Dances of the Heads), *Sol de Meio Dia* (Mid-day Sun), which he dedicated to the Xingu, and *Duas Vozes* (Two Voices) (Gilman 1998).

Milton Nascimento's 1990 CD *Txai!* was intended to raise awareness of the culture of Amazonian indigenous groups and the destruction of the Amazonian forest. It includes recordings of music by indigenous groups and a spoken discourse in English by actor River Phoenix.

The joint appearances by British rock star Sting and the Kayapó leader Raoni are not the only collaborations between Indian and non-Indian rock musicians. The Brazilian metal band Sepultura recorded the song "Itsari" for its CD *Roots* (1996) in a Xavante village in Mato Grosso, and included field recordings and tribal sounds in "Kaiowas" on *Chaos A.D.* (1993).

Popular Music in the Amazon Region. Several styles of popular music from the large cities of the Amazon region have gained attention on the national and international level, including *carimbó,* which originated as a dance performed by Brazilians of African descent on Marajó Island, near Belém, the capital of Pará state. As a pop style, it was associated with the singer Fafá de Belém in the 1970s. The international *lambada* craze in 1989 and 1990 was based on the appropriation by a French group of rhythms and compositions that had been played in Belém for years beforehand. (See McGowan and Pessanha, 1998: 154–7, for more information.) The Caribbean musical influences that were heard in the *lambada* are also present in the *guitarrada,* a guitar-based style from Belém. The *Mestres da Guitarrada,* a group formed by three guitarists with many years of experience playing the style, has recently recorded a CD and performed at the Rec-Beat festival in Recife. The guitarist Pio Lobato and his group Cravo Carbono have recorded songs inspired by the *guitarrada.* Boi-Bumbá, a form of the traditional *bumba-meu-boi* (see Chapter 4), has grown into a large-scale popular tradition in which competition between performing groups attracts huge audiences to Parintins, a town of 80,000 located on an island in the Amazon River, approximately 250 miles from Manaus, the capital of Amazonas state in northern Brazil.

CHAPTER 4

The Sound of the Northeast

Northeast Brazil includes the states of Maranhão, Piauí, Ceará, Rio Grande do Norte, Paraíba, Pernambuco, Alagoas, Sergipe, and Bahia. But like other regions of Brazil, it is more than a geographical area. The cultivation of sugarcane on plantations that used slave labor in the colonial period through the late nineteenth century established patterns of social stratification and expressive culture whose legacy is still visible today. In the twentieth century, the rapid industrialization of southern Brazil made the Northeast seem like an economic backwater by comparison. The Northeast is the site of periodic droughts that send thousands of people on migrations to seek better living conditions. It is also viewed as a repository of cultural traditions, especially musical ones, which, together with the many historical sites found there and the natural beauty of the region's beaches, have made the Northeast an important center of tourism. This chapter presents three examples of the sound of the Northeast in order to demonstrate the role of music in expressing a sense of regional identity: *cavalo-marinho, maracatu,* and *baião* and *forró.*

BUMBA-MEU-BOI AND *CAVALO-MARINHO*: THE DRAMA OF THE MAGICAL OX

All over Brazil there are versions of a folk performance about a magical ox (*boi*), which is generically called *bumba-meu-boi.* In some of them, the ox dies and is resurrected; in others, the ox sickens and is cured. Gathered around this dramatic nucleus are characters that represent the human, animal, and imaginary inhabitants of a plantation. The human characters include workers (who are portrayed as slaves in some versions), bosses, soldiers, tradesmen, cowboys, clowns, Indian shamans, husbands, wives. There are also animal characters, including an ox, a

FIGURE 4.1 Cavalo-marinho banco *of Mestre Batista. L to R: Sidrak,* mineiro; *Mané Roque,* bage; *Biu Roque,* bage; *Deodato,* pandeiro; *Luiz Paixão,* rabeca; *Mestre Batista.* *(Photo by John Murphy.)*

horse, a jaguar, and various birds, and imaginary ones, such as forest monsters, a dead man carrying a live one, and the devil.

Bumba-meu-boi takes various forms. In Maranhão state, the Boi groups have grown to rival Carnaval groups in size, and the peak of their season is St. John's Day, one of the three Catholic saints' days in June that are celebrated intensely in the North and Northeast (see Bueno 2001). In Santa Catarina, in the south, it is called *Boi de Mamão. Bumba-meu-boi* and *cavalo-marinho* are performed in Pernambuco and nearby states of Paraíba, Rio Grande do Norte, and Alagoas.

What distinguishes *cavalo-marinho* from *bumba-meu-boi* in Pernambuco is the musical repertory and instrumentation. In *cavalo-marinho,* the instrumental music is provided by *rabeca* (fiddle), *pandeiro* (tambourine), *bage* (or *reco-reco* [scraper]), and *mineiro* or *ganzá* (cylindrical rattle). In *bumba-meu-boi,* the instruments are *bombo* (small bass drum) and *ganzá.* The *cavalo-marinho* musicians are known collectively as the *banco,* after the bench that they sit on. Figure 4.1 shows the *banco* led by Mestre Batista.

Cavalo-marinho is not a genre that even most Brazilians are aware of, even though many are aware of *bumba-meu-boi* and the general outline of its plot. (The country is so large that many Brazilians have not visited regions that are distant from their own, and many depend on the mass media to construct their understanding of distant regions.) *Cavalo-marinho* is included in this book because its plot and vocal and instrumental music are interesting, it is a locally significant form of popular Catholic devotion, it expresses the moral worldview and comic sensibility of rural workers, and it is an unbroken oral tradition that reaches back to Portuguese celebrations of the Day of Kings (Epiphany). This traditional genre, which may seem unremarkable to those unacquainted with it, holds as much significance for its performers and audiences as the better-known Brazilian genres do for theirs. Readers can avoid confusion between *cavalo-marinho* and *bumba-meu-boi* in the sections that follow by remembering that *bumba-meu-boi* is the general name for a traditional performance genre that formed around the plot nucleus of the death and rebirth of an ox, and *cavalo-marinho* is the version of it that is practiced in Pernambuco and Paraíba, which borders it on the north.

Cavalo-marinho *Performers and Audiences.* *Cavalo-marinho* performances happen on Saturday nights during the sugarcane harvest season, from August through January. Most of the performers work in the cane fields, and their audiences include other agricultural workers and their families and other small town residents. Between harvests, the performers and their families survive on occasional work and what produce they can grow on their own small plots. In recent years, several large sugar processing plants have closed, making work harder to get even during the harvest season. Cutting sugarcane is hot, heavy, dangerous work. The fields are burned beforehand to clear away underbrush. The next day, the cutters enter the smoking fields and spend long days chopping, stacking, and loading the cane. The *cavalo-marinho* performers work a half day on Saturday, and their performances can last until dawn on Sunday, their one day off.

Some performers specialize as musicians or singers, as actors of roles such as that of Mateus, or as actors who can portray many of the dozens of characters in the repertory. Those who organize the groups and direct the performances are respectfully addressed as Mestre (master, or, more artistically, maestro).

Three Master Performers of Cavalo-marinho. Mestre Batista (1932–1991) (see Figure 4.1) represented a class of small landholders that was dwindling by the 1990s, as small cane-growing farms became uneconomical and had to be sold to large enterprises. He led the *maracatu* Estrela de Ouro as well as a *cavalo-marinho* group, and was known as a stern teacher who held his performers of traditional music and dance to standards of accuracy that would not be out of place in a conservatory. Batista was also deeply interested in popular poetry sold in markets as *folhetos* (booklets), which scholars call *literatura de cordel,* a reference to the string that the booklets are displayed on.

Mestre Manoel Salustiano (b. 1945), learned the *cavalo-marinho* tradition from his father and other *mestres* and eventually became highly skilled in other performance genres as well, including *maracatu de baque solto, mamulengo* (a Punch-and-Judy–style puppet show), and *ciranda* (a circle dance). He moved to Recife as a young man and remembers comparing his first sight of the ocean to the windswept cane fields back home. Salustiano and his family established themselves as expert performers of traditional music and dance and found patrons among the government and university community, which included Ariano Suassuna, the well-known poet, playwright, and scholar, and Leda Alves, who directed government cultural programs. After working in relative obscurity for years, Salustiano is today one of Recife's best-known cultural figures.

Mestre Inácio Lucindo da Silva (b. 1937) has spent his working life in the country, and continues to lead *cavalo-marinho* groups. He was born on a sugar plantation and drove oxen as a boy before starting to work in the cane. After learning *cavalo-marinho* by watching performances and eventually joining in, he formed his own group with coworkers from the cane fields while still in his teens and has led it ever since. He has struggled to provide for his family, and his work history is full of moves from one *engenho* (sugar plantation) to another, and from the plantations to the cities of the region and Rio de Janeiro, in search of better working and living conditions. He described his situation to me in 1996 as living with *uma canga no pescoço e uma faca no gogô* (a yoke on the neck and a knife at the throat), the "yoke" of hard physical work and the "knife" of hunger. With the increased interest in traditional music on the part of younger audiences starting in the mid-1990s, Inácio and other *mestres* of *cavalo-marinho* have found new opportunities to perform, while some of their old ones, like patron saint festivals or performances in the street, have become less numerous. In 2004, Inácio presented a workshop on *cavalo-marinho* at cultural centers and festivals in São Paulo state along with two young performer–researchers, Alício Amaral and Juliana Pardo.

Cavalo-marinho *Performance Contexts.* The performers have the most freedom to extend the performance to its full length at informal performances on small farms or on back streets of the cities and towns north of Recife. This type of performance is independent of a larger event, such as a town's patron saint festival, which would limit its duration and provide lots of amplified music to compete with the unamplified *cavaló-marinho. Cavalo-marinho* groups also perform at folkloric performances in Recife in which the night-long performance is shortened to one hour and a presenter helps to explain the performance to audiences that frequently include tourists.

Patron saint festivals combine religious processions and special masses with a carnival atmosphere. People come from neighboring towns, and people born in that town who live elsewhere come back for the occasion. Other performances presented at such a festival include *mamulengo; ciranda; forró,* in both *pé-de-serra* and *estilizado* styles (see below); *trios elétricos,* and temporary dance clubs featuring international pop hits.

A Cavalo-marinho *Performance.* At 9 p.m. on a Saturday night in December 1990, a group of men and boys has converged on a bar on a side street in a small town in the sugarcane-growing region outside of Recife, in the northeastern state of Pernambuco. They have come from their homes on outlying farms and other small towns to perform *cavalo-marinho.*

The outline of the plot is the following: first there is a warm-up dance to music played on the *rabeca* (fiddle), *pandeiro* (tambourine) (see Figure 4.1), *bage* (a bamboo scraper), and *mineiro* (a cylindrical metal rattle). Then a character named Mestre Ambrósio enters the circular performance area in front of the musicians and imitates each of the characters for the Capitão (Captain), who directs the performance. Mateus and Bastião, two comic herdsmen who have been left in control of the Captain's land, animate the proceedings with jokes and loud whacks from inflated ox bladders. They struggle with a Soldier, who wants them to give permission for the Captain to return. Once they give it, the performance proceeds with dances in honor of the Three Kings (Figure 4.2), continues with a long series of individual characters who represent outlaws, Indians, and fantastic animals, interspersed with improvised songs, and ends with a magical Ox, which dances, gets sick, and is revived as dawn breaks.

The first dramatic high point involves Mateus and Sebastião, two rural workers who have been left in control of a plantation by the

FIGURE 4.2 *Galante (left) and Dama dance during a performance of cavalo-marinho.* (*Photo by Jason Gardner.*)

Capitão, its absentee owner. The Capitão wants to return to his property, but Mateus and Sebastião resist (Figure 4.3), so the owner hires a Soldier to extract the permission by force. Mateus, Sebastião (or Bastião), and Catirina (the wife of one or the other—or both, in some versions—who is played by a man) are imagined to live in the time of slavery. The following song lyric makes this plain:

Catirina, minha nega	Catirina, my black woman
Meu senhor vai te vender	My master wants to sell you
Tu entra pro rio dos peixes	You'll go down the river of the fish
Nunca mais ninguém te ver	No one will ever see you again

The struggle for control of land within the performance reflects the real struggle that the performers face in their daily lives. The region is dominated by large landholdings, some owned by individuals and oth-

FIGURE 4.3 *In a performance of* cavalo-marinho *by Mestre Salustiano's group in Recife in 1989, the Soldado (Soldier, left) struggles with Mateus and Bastião.* *(Photo by John Murphy.)*

ers by the sugar corporations. The abundant supply of labor and the lack of other work options keep wages low. Brazilian law allows unproductive lands to be given to landless people, typically after a long legal process. *Cavalo-marinho* performers have been among those occupying such lands under the auspices of the *Movimento dos Sem-Terra,* the national movement of the landless. Before the 1960s, most sugarcane workers in this region resided on the plantations and worked in exchange for a house and a plot of land. Starting in the 1960s, they were evicted or left on their own in order to live under fewer constraints in town. Once they began working for wages, they lost access to the land that would allow them to plant their own crops to carry them through the between-harvest seasons. The towns where *cavalo-marinho* is performed are part of the same region in which anthropologist Nancy Scheper-Hughes did the research on infant mortality that forms the basis for her book *Death Without Weeping: the Violence of Everyday Life in Brazil* (1992).

Once the permission has been forced out of Mateus and Bastião, the Capitão celebrates his return with a party that also serves as a devotion to the *Divino Santo Rei do Oriente,* who represents either Jesus or (when the expression is in the plural) the *Reis Magos* (Three Kings). The peak of the *cavalo-marinho* performance season is Epiphany, January 6, when the Kings reached Bethlehem, just as it is for the Folia de Reis in southern Brazil (discussed in Chapter 5).

ACTIVITY 4.1 *The* toada *"Que estrela é aquela," a song in honor of the Divino Santo Rei do Oriente, on CD track 7, is sung by Mestre Inácio Lucindo da Silva (Figure 4.4). It expresses popular Catholic devotion to the Three Kings. After you listen to this song and follow its strophic form (new lyrics for the same tune), do some research on popular Catholicism in Brazil and elsewhere in Latin America to find out how it differs from the official Church doctrines and why such differences developed.*

Que estrela é aquela	What star is that
que alumeia lá no mar,	Which shines there on the sea
que alumeia lá no mar	
É o Divino Santo Rei	It's the Divine Holy King
Que nós viemos festejar	Whom we have come to celebrate
Que nos viemos festejar	
Oi viva Santo Rei	Long live the Holy King
Viva	
Santo Rei do Oriente	The Holy King of the East
Viva	
Que estrela é aquela	Which star is that
Que vem da parte do norte	Which comes from the north?
É o Divino Santo Rei	It's the Divine Holy King
Viemos dar a boa sorte	We've come to give good luck
Oi viva santo rei, etc.	

The song on CD track 7 demonstrates the Portuguese origins of this part of *cavalo-marinho,* since similar songs are contained in Portuguese

FIGURE 4.4 *Mestre Inácio sings a toada at his house in Condado, Pernambuco, 1996.* (Photo by John Murphy.)

folk song collections. It is sung by the Capitão and his Galantes, a sort of honor guard, with comic refrains by Mateus and Sebastião. Mateus can be heard singing "*o prefeito de Condado*" (the mayor of Condado, the town where the performance is taking place), which is comic because he is mixing the local and mundane with a religious song.

The song for the Capitão on his horse describes the horse as a *cavalo-marinho*, or marine horse, a term which some performers think described a special horse imported by the Portuguese (hence marine, from over the sea) that knew special gaits. *Cavalo-marinho* is also the Portuguese word for the sea horse, but this has nothing to do with the performance.

Cavalo-marinho dança muito bem	*Cavalo-marinho* dances very well
Cavalo-marinho dança muito bem	
Já pode chamar	Now it can be called
Marica meu bem	Marica, my love

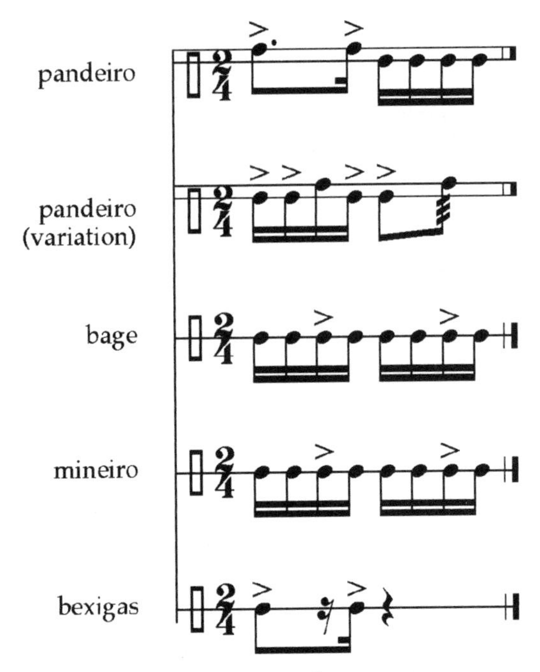

FIGURE 4.5 Cavalo-marinho *percussion.*

Between scenes, Mestre Inácio sings *toadas soltas,* songs that are not connected to a character, and includes improvised lyrics that share news and comment on the performance and those in attendance. The *toadas* alternate with *baianos* played by the *rabequeiro* (*rabeca* player). *Baiano* is related to the *baião,* which Luiz Gonzaga transformed into a nationally known genre. Both share a rhythmic emphasis on the downbeat and the last sixteenth note of the first beat (if the meter is thought of as a quick 2/4). Figure 4.5 shows the basic percussion patterns used in *cavalo-marinho.* The first *pandeiro* pattern is like the one played by the late Manoel Deodato; the second is like the one played by Mestre Inácio. The line labeled *bexigas* shows the rhythm of the inflated ox bladders played by Mateus and Sebastião.

ACTIVITY 4.2 *As you listen to CD track 8, Inácio's* toada *"Inácio quando morrer," notice the way the* rabeca *part supports the vocal line. Follow the lyrics in translation.*

Inácio quando morrer	When Inácio dies
Vai beber na venda nova	He'll drink at the new store
Inácio quando morrer	When Inácio dies
Plantado debaixo da cova	Planted beneath the grave
Só peço quando eu morrer	I ask only that when I die
Me enterro neste terreiro	That I'm buried under this ground
Me bota um braço de fora	Leave one of my arms out
Pra eu pegar neste pandeiro	So I can grab this pandeiro
O beber me alegra muito	Drinking makes me very happy
O fumar me dá prazer	Smoking gives me pleasure
Quem não fuma e quem não bebe	He who doesn't smoke or drink
Que alegria pode ter?	What joy can he have?

The first verse, which is probably a formula, is reminiscent of the postmortem instructions in blues lyrics such as "See That My Grave Is Kept Clean" by Blind Lemon Jefferson. At the conclusion of the second verse, Mateus yells "iêeeeee," which is similar to the yells heard in rodas de capoeira. *(Inácio, by the way, does not drink to excess or smoke; in another improvised verse he sings "eu brinco sem beber" [I perform without drinking]).*

The rabeca *is a folk fiddle of Portuguese origin. Its four strings are tuned in fifths, like those of the violin, but the tuning is variable depending on the pitch of the vocal music it accompanies or the taste of the player. The neck is somewhat shorter than that of the violin, and the playing position supports the bottom of the instrument on the player's chest. For more on this instrument, see Murphy (1997).*

∞

FIGURE 4.6 *Luiz Paixão (Luiz Alves Ferreira), widely regarded as the foremost* rabequeiro *of* cavalo-marinho. *Pictured at the University of Florida, Gainesville, where he performed during the "Staging Identities" conference in 2000.* (Photo by *John Murphy.*)

ACTIVITY 4.3 *As you listen to CD track 9,* rabeca baianos *by Luiz Paixão (Figure 4.6), follow the notations. The first pair of tunes are variations on these four-measure outlines (Figure 4.7).*

Then Paixão plays a theme that was a special favorite of Mestre Batista. My transcription does not notate the open strings that he plays along with melody notes (Figure 4.8). Note the timing of the shift to this theme.

As dawn breaks, after a long series of characters has entered the *roda* (performance circle), the *Boi* (ox) enters. One of the *cavalo-marinho* ac-

FIGURE 4.7 *Musical example* rabeca baianos, *1.*

tors wears the large, heavy costume made with a real ox's skull and horns. He wheels and lunges, scattering the laughing audience members (Figure 4.9). Then he sickens and has to be cured by the Doctor.

The songs sung at any given point in *cavalo-marinho* differ from one group to the next. I have included two examples from this point in the drama. CD track 10 was sung by Mestre Inácio's group on December 2, 1990.

Meu boi estava descansando	My ox was resting
No sombro do meio-dia	In the shade of midday
Quando ele abriu os olhos	When he opened his eyes
Viu o velho Vicente Maria	He saw old Vicente Maria
Com a guiada na mão	With his staff in his hand
Dizendo no coração	Saying from his heart

FIGURE 4.8 *Musical example* rabeca baianos, *2.*

FIGURE 4.9 *Mateus (right) raises his bexiga (inflated ox bladder) to strike the dancing Boi as Bastião looks on in a performance of cavalo-marinho.* (Photo by Jason Gardner.)

Foi eu que botou no chão	It was I who put you on the ground
Oi lá morreu, lá morreu	Oh there he died, there he died
Lá morreu, camaleão	There he died, chameleon

CD track 11 was sung by Mestre Batista's group in a recording session at his house on May 19, 1991. It features an extraordinary vocal duo, that of the late Manoel Deodato, who sang in a powerful baritone and had a fast and strong style on the *pandeiro*, and Biu Roque, who is a part of Siba's group Fuloresta do Samba, who sings an octave above. (Figure 4.10).

Sapo cururu	Cururu frog
Da beira do rio	On the riverbank
Quando o sapo canta, ô sadona	When the frog sings, oh milady
Cururu tem frio	The *cururu* (a bird) is cold
Eh, boi!	
Foi a cobra verde	It was the green snake
Dentro do capim	In the tall grass
Que mordeu meu boi, ô sadona	That bit my ox, oh milady

FIGURE 4.10 *Photo of* Cavalo-marinho *singers Biu Roque, left, and Manoel Deodato.* (*Photo by John Murphy.*)

Que será de mim?	What will become of me?
Eh, boi!	
Sapatero novo	Young shoemaker
Me faz um sapato	Make me a shoe
Da sola bem fina, sadona	With a thin sole, milady
Do salto bem alto	And a high heel
Eh, boi!	
Pra dançar no salto	To dance on the heel
Dança muito bem	Dances very well
Já mandei chamar, ô senhora	I already had him called, milady
Marica, meu bem	Marica, my dear
Eh, boi!	

[the excerpt fades then continues]

Se meu boi morrer	If my ox should die
Que será de mim?	What will become of me?
Manda buscar outro, ô senhora	Send for another one, oh milady
Lá em Surubim	There in Surubim
Eh, boi!	

Sometimes the *Boi* does not survive and is ceremonially slaughtered. In the December 1990 performance by Mestre Inácio's group, it rose and danced some more, and then the performance ended with a round of "Viva!"s and a song whose lyrics made political references—to the Liberal Alliance of the 1930s.

Cavalo-marinho *Today.* When I studied *cavalo-marinho* in 1990–1991, it was little known outside of the communities where it was performed and the urban community of traditional music scholars and enthusiasts (see Murphy 1994). Like other traditional performance genres, it received some support from city and state cultural agencies. During the intervening years, there has been a tremendous increase in the interest of the younger generation in traditional music, dance, and theater. Siba, whose *maracatu* is discussed below, learned to play *rabeca* extremely well and to sing the *cavalo-marinho* repertoire (see Figure 4.11). When he formed the band Mestre Ambrósio, he brought public attention to the *rabeca* and to the *cavalo-marinho, maracatu,* and *coco* traditions that the band drew on for its original music. Other young musicians have learned these traditions as well. See the web site for details.

This renewed interest has brought benefits to the traditional performers who live in the country and continue to work in agriculture but still face significant economic hardships. Siba and others, including a new generation of Brazilian graduate students who combine research with performance (such as André Bueno, Gustavo Vilar, and Maria Acselrad), continue to advocate for more public recognition of the value of traditional genres like *cavalo-marinho* and the people who sustain them. *Cavalo-marinho* expresses popular religious devotion, and it dramatizes the struggle over land that is a crucial element of daily life in the region. It is a source of aesthetic pleasure: the pleasure one finds in the tunes and lyrics of the *toadas* and *baianos,* in the costumes and dances, in a well-told joke, and the pleasure of spending a night in the open air, after a week of hard work, surrounded by one's friends and making music.

MARACATU: AFRO-BRAZILIAN CARNIVAL GENRE WITH A SACRED SIDE

Maracatu is a traditional performance genre that exists in two forms in Pernambuco. *Maracatu de nação* (nation *maracatu*), also called *maracatu de baque virado* (turned-around beat *maracatu*), is associated with Afro-Brazilian religious centers in the city of Recife. It resembles the royal procession of an African nation, and the instrumental music that accompanies its singing music is dominated by the sound of powerful bass drums called *alfaia*, snare drums, and a two-toned metal bell playing a medium-slow, heavily syncopated beat.

Maracatu rural (rural *maracatu*), also called *maracatu de baque solto* (loose-beat *maracatu*), is practiced in the rural areas surrounding Recife. It resembles a colorful warlike procession and blends Afro-Brazilian and indigenous elements in its underlying belief system and costumes. The vocal music typically consists of composed and improvised verses by two master singers in friendly competition, accompanied by a small brass ensemble and a percussion group consisting of snare drums, metal bell, and *cuíca* that plays a fast rhythm that might remind contemporary listeners of drum and bass.

I first saw *maracatu* on Saturday, November 24, 1990, at Mestre Batista's small farm at Chã de Camará, outside of Aliança, a small town in the sugar-growing region of Pernambuco. It was not a "performance" of *maracatu*—this was not something staged for an audience—but a *sambada*, a meeting between two *mestres* (in this context, poet–singers), Juruti do Norte and Cigarra do Norte, their *ternos* (instrumental ensembles), and the men and women who would be part of each *maracatu*'s upcoming Carnaval appearance. (Notice the word *sambada*, derived from the verb *sambar*, to play music and dance, which relates to the word *samba*.) I went there with Mestre Salustiano, Siba, and members of Salustiano's family and his *maracatu*. It was sugarcane harvest season. We passed heavily loaded cane trucks on the way there, and smelled sugar cane being burned in the fields and processed in factories.

***A* Sambada.** In the early part of the evening, Mestre Juruti do Norte sang a series of verses, beginning with a *marcha* in four-line *quadras* and progressing to *samba* in ten lines. Circled about him were the members of the *terno*, who played *bombo* (small bass drum), *tarol* (snare drum), valve trombone, *gongué* (a large double bell), and *mineiro* (cylindrical metal rattle). During the poetic declamations, the *terno* was silent. Between them, it burst into a fast beat with syncopated rhythms on top of steady sixteenth notes, against which the trombonist played a marchlike melody.

ACTIVITY 4.4 *The recording* "maracatu *percussion*" *provides an example of the instrumental interlude between Juruti do*

Norte's verses. It can be heard at my website. (The poetry of maracatu *will be discussed below.) In repeated listenings, try to follow the basic part of each instrument in the notation on the website. Two variants are shown for the* bombo *part, one for the* gongué. *The basic parts are always varied in performance.*

Later in the evening, Mestre Juruti was joined by Mestre Cigarra do Norte and a second group, Maracatu Leão de Ouro from Upatininga, a nearby town, playing a memorable march theme.

ACTIVITY 4.5 *As you listen to* "Marcha *played at* maracatu sambada," *which can be heard on my web site, pay attention to the theme and the percussion accompaniment and listen for the* mestre's *whistle and the* caboclo de lança's chocalhos *(rattles), which clank in the slower rhythm of the steps of the* caboclo de lança *(a warrior figure in* maracatu*). After the visiting* maracatu *is announced, the accompaniment pauses. The* mestre *sings verses using the same tune as the instrumental* marcha *and male voices and the female voices of the* baianas *respond, the latter straining to sing in their highest register. The second verse is "e responda satisfeito, aonde é que eu vou ficar" (and tell me in a satisfied way, where I will remain). Then the instrumental* marcha *and percussion return.*

The two groups' exchanges continued on through the night, as the women who would fill the roles of *baiana* sang the refrains and the men who would fill the roles of *caboclo-de-pena* (a figure in *maracatu* distinguished by a tall feathered headdress) and *caboclo-de-lança* danced on the packed earth in front of Mestre Batista's house.

At the *sambada* in November 1990, a few *caboclos-de-lança* were already preparing for Carnaval by wearing their *surrão*, a heavy frame on their back with four large metal rattles attached, and carrying their *guiada*, an 8-foot lance.

ACTIVITY 4.6 *Because the sound of the* caboclo de lança *is a unique part of the soundscape of the Mata Norte of Pernambuco, it is worth listening to an example that isolates the sound. Using the recording found on my web site, listen to the sound of the rattles as two* caboclos de lança *pass by, with the music of the* terno *in the background. The rattles of the second* caboclo *are pitched lower.*

Maracutu *Rural*. When I attended this *sambada* in 1990, I already knew that this was one of the two main types of *maracatu* practiced in Pernambuco. I also knew that both types were prominent parts of Carnaval as practiced in Recife and that many of the performers of *cavalo-marinho* were also members of *maracatu rural* groups. What I did not know was how rich, deep, and mostly hidden to outsiders the world of *maracatu rural* is. Since then, I have heard it many more times and learned more about its traditions, but I still cannot claim to understand it from the inside. In the following paragraphs, I shall discuss the origin and content of *maracatu* and describe its recent resurgence. Then I shall present an example composed and performed by Siba, the person from whom I have learned most about *maracatu*, and his collaborator, whose artistic name is Barachinha. In the discussion that follows, *maracatu* will refer to *maracatu rural* unless otherwise specified.

Maracatu is related to the African-derived traditions of Cambinda and Aruenda, and to the syncretic belief system known as *Jurema Sagrada* (Sacred *Jurema*), which combines Afro-Brazilian practices such as spirit possession, Amerindian spiritual practices, and popular Catholicism, a diverse set of religious traditions cultivated by believers without the involvement of clergy. It also draws on the characters (such as Mateus and Catirina from the *bumba-meu-boi*) and poetry (such as the four- and ten-line verse forms) of the dramatic dances of the region, which are transformations of traditional practices from Portugal. Two musical genres that are also practiced, separately, are found within *maracatu* presentations as well: *coco*, a responsorial song and dance accompanied by percussion and hand claps, and *ciranda*, a circle dance accompanied by snare drum with brass or saxophone refrains.

The *caboclo de lança* is at once the most public and the most mysterious symbol of *maracatu*. The carnation that he carries in his mouth represents a secret. He is said to fortify himself for the rigors of Carnaval with a potion called *azougue* made from sugarcane rum, cooking oil, and gunpowder and to spend long periods in a trance.

By the late nineteenth century, *maracatu* had developed into something like its present form. It flourished in the countryside around Recife until the 1960s and 1970s, when changes in the sugar industry weakened many rural communities and, as a result, the traditional genres practiced by rural workers. Since the 1990s, there has been a resurgence of interest in *maracatu* and an increase in participation in them by young people, which was inspired by the *mangue* movement (see Chapter 6) and by the continuing work of artists, like Mestre Salustiano, who present traditional genres to new audiences.

The two kinds of *maracatu, rural* and *de nação*, are the most prominent genres of Carnaval in Recife and Olinda (see Guerra-Peixe 1980 and Real 1990). They far outnumber the *escolas de samba* and the other regional genres represented in Carnaval, which include the Amerindian-influenced *caboclinhos* and the *bois de carnaval*, a form of *bumba-meu-boi*. Today, there are more than eighty *maracatu rural* groups, which have formed a governing organization in order to negotiate the terms of their participation in Carnaval (Oliveira Pinto 1996).

In December 2000, the first festival of *maracatu rural* was held in Nazaré da Mata, a small city outside Recife. Joatan Vilela Berbel, an official of the national Ministry of Culture, was present for the event and was interviewed about the importance of local culture in the context of globalization:

> [Luiz Joaquim, journalist]: Is it possible to be competitive [in the national and international cultural marketplace] with just local culture?
>
> [Joatan Vilela Berbel]: It's necessary to take advantage of globalization, which people are talking about so much. That's where government can play a role, by supporting projects such as Pernambuco in Concert, conceived by Africa Productions [a Recife organization that promotes local culture, and which produced the CD *Maracatu Atômico*, with includes both kinds of *maracatu*]. Once you're able to produce a CD, put materials on the Internet, and publicize them internationally, a demand will automatically arise for the simple reason that no one in the world produces *maracatu*, and no one will ever be able to produce legitimate *maracatu* outside of Pernambuco.
>
> [Joaquim]: Can't globalization function in the opposite way, as a degenerating force on popular culture?
>
> [Berbel]: Yes, but even this has a positive side. If not for this imminent danger, this alert, perhaps we wouldn't be as interested in us-

> ing regional culture as a basis for our self-esteem [in the original, *auto-valorização*, self-valuing, a stronger expression than "self-esteem," which in Portuguese is *auto-estima*], as we are now (Joaquim 2000).

Siba and Barachinha's "Catimbó." Siba is the artistic name of Sérgio Veloso, a musician from Pernambuco. He began playing and singing traditional music while a music student at the Federal University of Pernambuco. After becoming highly proficient on the *rabeca* and learning the entire *cavalo-marinho* repertoire, he formed the band Mestre Ambrósio, its music inspired by traditional *forró* played on the *rabeca* and button accordion, *cavalo-marinho, maracatu rural,* and *coco,* with strong elements of Afro-Brazilian percussion. Beginning in the early 1990s, Siba began participating in *maracatu rural* and learning the art of improvised poetry from older *mestres.*

His project *Fuloresta do samba* (Forest—in the local pronunciation—of samba) is a collaboration with several generations of musicians in the Zona da Mata Norte. He released a CD by that title in 2002, and in 2003 released the collaboration with Barachinha, a younger mestre, entitled *No baque solto somente* (Only in the *baque solto* style), from which CD track 12 is drawn. The following comments from Siba's liner notes to *Fuloresta do samba* convey the spirit of these collaborations.

> [This project] was born out of my uneasiness about the way traditional music (with the sometimes pejorative label of *folklore*) is always considered more of an amusement than an art, a frozen past that can only serve as a reference for the present, "modern" time. This common sense notion contrasts radically with the dynamic reality of a region that is extremely poor, but possesses a popular culture that's diversified and always in motion, according to the changes that time brings. *Fuloresta do samba* is our attempt to interfere in the present, revering the past and projecting a future (Siba 2002).

Siba's current projects include a 6-CD series entitled *Poetas do Norte,* which documents the poetry and song of the Zona da Mata Norte, and a documentary film about the *Fuloresta do samba* project.

ACTIVITY 4.7 *CD track 12 presents "Catimbó," by Siba and Barachinha; the complete lyrics can be found on the web site. The track opens with the* mestres' *whistles and the brass melody and percussion of the* terno; *listen for the* póica *(friction drum).*

FIGURE 4.11 *Siba (left), Barachina.* *(Photo by Gilvan Barreto, Agência Lumiar de Fotugrafia, www.lumiarfoto.com.br.)*

Then Siba starts an alternating series of verses in the form of samba de dez linhas *(ten-line* samba*). The rhyme scheme is noted in the column between the Portuguese original and the English translation. As you listen, note the timing of the beginning and also of line 5 of each verse.*

A pouca ciência sua	A	Your small knowledge
Só deu para jogar bozó	B	Is only good for gambling
Apele pro catimbó	B	You appeal to *catimbó*

Que é pra ver se continua	A	To see whether to continue
Se um mestre bom lhe autua	A	If a good *mestre* possesses you
Você pensa que se inspira	C	You think you're inspired

[lines five and six are repeated]

Mas aí vem pomba-gira	C	But here comes *pomba-gira*
Em menos de um segundo	D	In less than a second
A pouca sorte no mundo	D	The little luck in the world
Que você tinha, ela tira	C	That you had, she takes away

After an instrumental interlude, Barachinha responds:

Se é pouca minha ciência	A	If my knowledge is small
Mas quando estou na batalha	B	When I'm in the battle
Dez mestres da sua igualha	B	Ten *mestres* as good as you
Não tem minha inteligência	A	Don't have my intelligence
Que quem não tem competência	A	Because incompetent singers
Canta ruim de fazer dó	C	Sing so badly it's painful

[lines five and six are repeated]

Tu só pensa em catimbó	C	You only think about *catimbó*
Inveja e praga maldita	D	Envy and evil spells
Só quem nada disso evita	D	Only those who avoid them
De eu lhe cortar de cipó	C	Will escape being cut by a vine

Then it is Siba's turn:

Soube que você correu	A	I heard you ran away
Pra se sentar no puleiro	B	To sit in the chicken coop
Da casa de um feiticeiro	B	At the house of a spiritist
Que seu dinheiro comeu	A	Who ate your money
E o meu nome escreveu	A	And wrote my name
Na boca de um cururu	C	In the mouth of a *cururu*

[lines five and six are repeated]

Deu garrafa de Pitu	C	Gave a bottle of sugarcane rum
Fez um despacho com bode	D	Made an offering of a goat
Mesmo assim você não pode	D	But even so you can't
Vencer-me maracatu	C	Beat my *maracatu*

And Barachinha responds:

Não procurei feiticeiro	A	I didn't look for a spiritist
Pra me ajudar na cantiga	B	To help me sing better
Que pra lhe vencer na briga	B	To beat you in a fight
Eu penso em Jesus primeiro	A	I think of Jesus first
Em vez de gastar dinheiro	A	Instead of wasting money
Com mentira e bruxaria	C	With lies and witchcraft

[lines five and six are repeated]

Que fazendo poesia	C	By making poetry
Na sua frente eu dou show	D	I put on a show right in front of you
Que cada passo que dou	D	Because every step I take
Levo Deus na companhia	C	I take God with me

[excerpt fades]

Notice how Siba and Barachinha make reference to key words in each other's verses, such as pouca ciência *(small knowledge) in the first pair of verses and* feiticeiro *(spiritist) in the second. In the verses Siba sings after this excerpt, he (or rather his poetic persona) continues to threaten Barachinha with misfortune from* catimbó *curses that will lead Barachinha into slavery. His only recourse is to join the evangelical church. Barachinha's verses maintain his resistance, supported by Christian faith. This tension between Catholicism and spiritism reflects similar tensions in Brazilian society in general. While Catholicism is historically the national religion, Protestant churches have grown rapidly in recent decades, and participation in Afro-Brazilian religions such as* candomblé *and various syncretic forms of spiritism is widespread.*

BAIÃO AND *FORRÓ*: ACCORDION-DRIVEN DANCE MUSIC

Music provides what is arguably the strongest and most widely recognized symbol of Northeastern regional identity. The *baião,* a dance rhythm introduced nationally by Luiz Gonzaga, the *forró* that developed from it, and eventually Gonzaga himself became a source of pride for Northeasterners and a source of strength and nostalgia as they migrated to the large cities of the South in search of better living conditions. *Baião* is the name given to the genre that is identified by the rhythm shown below in Figure 4.13 on page 97, with lyrics on Northeastern themes and accompaniment by accordion, *zabumba* (bass drum), and triangle. *Forró* is a more general term that is used in several ways: as a genre label to refer to uptempo *baião*; as an umbrella term for a family of Northeastern dance rhythms; as a label for a dance style; as a label for a dance or party at which these rhythms are performed; and as the name of a place where such a party takes place. The use of *forró* to refer both to uptempo *baião* and to a family of rhythms is comparable to the use of *salsa* to refer both to uptempo *son montuno* and to *mambo, guaracha, guajira, bomba, plena,* and other rhythms. The etymology of *forró* is subject to debate. Some authors claim that it comes from parties organized by British railroad companies for their Brazilian workers that were advertised as "for all." More plausible is its derivation from the Portuguese word *forrobodó,* which refers to a festive musical gathering and dates from before the presence of the British companies.

Luiz Gonzaga and the Baião. Luiz Gonzaga is the most important musical representative of the *sertão* in the history of Brazilian music. As outlined in Chapter 2, Northeastern music had been nationally popular in earlier decades: stylized Northeastern songs by Catulo da Paixão Cearense had become popular in the 1910s, and there was a brief vogue for groups such as the Turunas Pernambucanos in the 1920s. Then came the samba. Once it was accepted as the national music (complete with its roots in Bahian music from the Northeast), Northeastern music was relegated to the regional category and looked down upon by many urbanites for its lack of sophistication. When Luiz Gonzaga (Figure 4.12) gained national prominence in the 1940s, Brazil was in the midst of a wave of North American music, including movie musicals and big band swing. Through the force of his music, the directness of his lyrics, and the appeal of his persona, however, Gonzaga reminded Brazilians of the joys and sorrows of rural life that had done so much to shape the national character.

Luiz Gonzaga's life and career encompassed most of the twentieth century, offering a chance to review important trends in Brazilian popular music. He was born on December 13, 1912, in Exu, Pernambuco, a city located 753 miles inland from Recife. His father, Januário, worked

FIGURE 4.12 *Luiz Gonzaga.* *(Photo courtesy Contéudo Expresso, www.contentxp.com.)*

in agriculture and played the accordion for religious festivals, weddings, and *forrós*. Januário also repaired accordions, which was (and for many accordionists still is) a crucial skill especially when specialized repair technicians and the money to pay them were scarce.

By age twelve, Luiz was accompanying his father in performances in the cities and small towns of the *sertão* of Pernambuco, and by age fourteen he was performing on his own. He was able to attend school enough to become literate. In 1930, before his eighteenth birthday, he fell in love with the daughter of a local elite family and quarreled with her father, who had forbidden their romance on the grounds that Gonzaga was an accordionist with few prospects. After being strongly disciplined by his mother over the incident, he left town to join the Army, where he spent close to ten years. He played the accordion in miltitary bands, learned music theory, and learned the repertoire of polkas, waltzes, tangos, and foxtrots that were popular at the time. Staying in Rio de Janeiro when he left the Army in 1939, Gonzaga worked in the Mangue, a red-light district, and elsewhere in Rio.

In 1940 he began to appear on amateur shows on the radio, including on Ari Barroso's Rádio Tupi, without much success. Then he was asked by some students from Ceará, in the Northeast, to play music from that region. The reaction was enthusiastic. When he returned to the radio shows with this instrumental repertoire, it launched him on a career of broadcasting and recording. Because his voice quality and vocal style were different from the polished radio voices of the time, it took some time for his sound to be accepted.

In 1945, Gonzaga met the first of his two most important lyricist partners, Humberto Teixeira, a lawyer from Ceará. In 1946, the pair produced the song "Baião," which started (and named) the most significant musical trend since the samba and until the *bossa nova*. The rhythm emphasizes the pattern in Figure 4.13, which is reminiscent of the *baiano* heard in *cavalo-marinho* (see Figure 4.5). The rhythm on the top line is reinforced by chords on the accordion. The bottom rhythm is played on lower-pitched percussion instruments, such as the *zabumba*, and reinforced by the bass line.

The lyrics of "Baião" introduce the dance and argue for its superiority over other genres, including samba. The melody is supported by long stretches of dominant harmony, which must have created a distinct contrast with the faster-moving harmonies of the samba and North American standards that were popular around the same time. The song concludes with Gonzaga's falsetto singing that is reminiscent of the *aboio*, or cattle call.

FIGURE 4.13 Baião *rhythmic pattern.*

In 1947 Gonzaga and Teixeira composed "Asa Branca," which was a tremendous success and eventually came to be considered "the hymn of the Northeast." The lyrics are sung from the point of view of a *sertanejo,* who has to leave his land because of drought, and are addressed to Rosinha, the woman he is leaving behind. This dramatizes an event that was all too common in real life in the drought-plagued interior of the Northeast. The lyrics are sung in the Northeastern dialect, which Gonzaga helped turn into a symbol of pride. The musical form is strophic with an instrumental refrain. The third and fourth lines of each four-line stanza of text are repeated.

ACTIVITY 4.8 *Search the web for lyrics to "Asa Branca" and its English translation and a legal download of the song in its entirety or an excerpt. Better yet, see if your library has Gonzaga's original recording. Listen for the sound of the accordion,* zabumba, *and triangle and follow the narrative of the lyrics.*

By 1949 Gonzaga was a national star. He wrote successful songs in partnership with Teixeira and with lyricist José Dantas, including "Vem Morena" and "A Dança da Moda." He spent the 1950s touring all over Brazil and recording dozens of songs that have become standards in the *forró* repertoire. Luiz Gonzaga and the *baião* played a role in Brazilian music similar to that of the blues in the formation of rock 'n' roll in the United States. It was not so much a rejection of the urbane sophistication of *samba-canção* and U.S. popular songs popular in Brazil at the time; after all, Gonzaga knew that repertoire, too. It was a reassertion of a more direct style of expression that had never gone out of style among the masses of Brazilians who lived far from large urban centers. By speaking in the language of the interior, by singing in a voice that occasionally cracked with emotion, by playing the accordion, the instrument that animated countless country dances, and by dressing in the leather gear of the backlands cowboy, Gonzaga created a national voice for the other Brazil, the one that would never set foot in a Rio de Janeiro casino. Gonzaga remained faithful to this musical ideal and to his role as a spokesman for the *sertanejo* throughout his career. His visual image, with its elaborately tooled leather clothes and hat, plus his constant companion the accordion, became a national icon.

With the popularity of *bossa nova*, Gonzaga's national popularity declined, but he remained "O Rei do Baião" (The King of the *Baião*) for audiences in the interior. He continued to compose and record new songs with a variety of collaborators, despite car accidents and thefts of his accordion. In 1967 he acknowledged his illegitimate son, known as Gonzaguinha, who went on to have a significant musical career of his own. In the late 1960s, Gilberto Gil and Caetano Veloso, leaders of the *Tropicália* movement, publicly asserted his importance. Veloso included "Asa Branca" on an album he recorded while in political exile in London. The song became a symbol of those who were opposed to the military government, though Gonzaga himself was criticized for giving the regime his partial support. He collaborated on the creation of the *Missa do Vaqueiro* (Cowboy Mass), which protested the oppression of Northeasterners.

In the 1970s, Gonzaga returned to national prominence. He was the subject of retrospective TV specials, and his song "Capim Novo" was used on the soundtrack for a TV Globo *telenovela*, a reliable sign of popularity. He returned to his hometown and helped to preserve the *asa branca* bird and to bring peace to feuding families. His importance for Brazilian music continued to be recognized throughout the 1980s. He performed abroad and collaborated on recordings with Gonzaguinha, accordionist Dominguinhos, and singers Elba Ramalho, Alceu Valença, Raimundo Fagner, Milton Nascimento, and Gal Costa. He continued to be active until shortly before his death, in Recife on August 2, 1989. His funeral drew thousands of mourners to the streets of Recife, Juazeiro do Norte (where he was blessed at the memorial for Padre Cícero), and Exu. At his burial, a gathering of 20,000 people sang "Asa Branca." Luiz Gonzaga's music remains a part of Brazilian music in the present. Posthumous releases and re-releases of his recordings on CD are widely available, and his songs have been recorded (and remixed) by many other artists.

Luiz Gonzaga's Music and the Invention of the Northeast. Luiz Gonzaga's music articulated the nostalgia felt by Northeastern migrants to the large cities of the south, a migration comparable to the Great Migration of African-Americans in the United States from the rural south to large northern cities during the first half of the twentieth century. In the Brazilian case, those coming from coastal cities tended to be Afro-Brazilian, while those who came from the interior tended to be *mestiço* (Portuguese-Indian-African heritage, in various combinations). Gonzaga's music being broadcast nationally on radio and distributed on records helped create the image of the region as the place of nostalgia and the past. In a study of the invention of the concept of the Northeast of Brazil, historian Durval Muniz de Albuquerque, Jr., writes of the importance of radio in the 1940s in general and Gonzaga's music and image in particular in both promoting national identity and revealing the diversity of the country (1999: 152). Every aspect of Gonzaga's presentation carried symbolic importance: the dance rhythms of the *baião*, the stylized leather clothing of the *sertão* horseman, the nostalgic lyrics, and most of all his voice quality and accent (1999: 155), which reached radio listeners through the spoken passages on his recordings. Northeasterners in southern cities revealed their origins as soon as they began to speak, and they encountered negative stereotypes and discrimination. When Gonzaga's voice and accent were acclaimed as symbols of an authentic Brazil, all Northeasterners were able to take more pride in their heritage.

Along with these positive effects, however, Albuquerque argues, Gonzaga's music contributed to the invention of the Northeast as the land of the past, of drought, of hard rural labor. By an invention, I do not mean something fake or phony, but a musical and stage persona that is consciously crafted and maintained to communicate certain cultural meanings and not others. Gonzaga's music is an example of the invention of the Northeast because the timeless vision of the region that it evokes is actually a modern creation, dependent on sophisticated urban musical production and lyrics, radio, and commercial distribution, and it helps to blend the diverse local traditions of the Northeast into a single entity.

> His music helped to reinforce the perception of the Northeast as a unity and a separate space in the country, a homogeneity conceived in opposition to the South. It reinforces not only the regional identity of his public, but the identity between them and their "region," and between him and his people, living "outside of their land" (Albuquerque 1999: 161).

By creating so vivid an image of the Northeast as the region of traditional rural culture as opposed to the modern life of the large cities of the south, he may have helped to confine Northeasterners in a way of thinking about themselves that reinforced negative stereotypes.

Arlindo dos Oito Baixos and Instrumental Forró. During the June patron saint festivals known collectively as São João, or the Festas Juninas, *forró* is as omnipresent as *samba* is during Carnaval season. The Catholic feast days devoted to Saint Anthony (June 13), Saint John (June

24), and Saint Peter (June 29) are celebrated in neighborhood parties that feature mock country weddings, square dances, bonfires, and open-air *forró* dances. In huge nightclubs, bands play stylized *forró* using electronic keyboards and drum sets along with the traditional accordion, *zabumba* (bass drum), and triangle. Stylized *forró* has begun to occupy more space on radio playlists and the CD market than the traditional style. Much of this kind of *forró* is produced in Ceará, and many of the seemingly interchangeable bands from there have food-related names, such as Mastruz com Leite (*mastruz*, a medicinal herb, with milk), one of the best-known *forró* bands from that state. An even more pop-sounding substyle is practiced by groups such as Falamansa in south-central Brazil.

Traditional *forró*, however, continues to thrive. Called *pé-de-serra* (literally "at the foot of the mountain"), it is played in the style of Luiz Gonzaga and the trios that play for country dances, with instrumental accompaniment by accordion, *zabumba*, and triangle. Recife and Caruaru, in Pernambuco, and Campina Grande, in Paraíba, are strongholds of the *pé-de-serra* style.

The *forró* parties in the small club that Arlindo dos Oito Baixos has built behind his house in Dois Unidos, an outlying neighborhood of Recife, have a more intimate feel than the huge nightclubs and São João street parties, and they show that *forró* is more than a seasonal music. All year long the Sunday evening parties attract an audience of neighbors, local *forró* enthusiasts, students, and foreign tourists. The best players and singers of *forró* and especially accordionists spend their nights off there. Each Sunday's lineup features several bands, including that of the host, Arlindo dos Oito Baixos, a virtuoso player of the *sanfona de oito baixos*, or eight-bass button accordion (Figure 4.14) The dance floor is crowded with couples dancing the quick *forró* two-step in a tight embrace. Understandably, the song repertoire features Luiz Gonzaga's music. Arlindo plays many instrumental *forró* tunes of his own composition along with *choros*, *frevos*, *xotes*, and *merengues*. Besides the accordion, his group includes *zabumba*, electric bass, triangle, *pandeiro* (tambourine), *ganzá* (metal rattle), and *agogô* (double metal bell).

Arlindo explains why he felt it necessary to turn his backyard into Recife's headquarters of *forró pé-de-serra*:

> My idea in making this *forró* is to bring together the musicians, the accordionists, and singers of *forró* and Northeastern music in general. Recife is a very large city, but it has few *forró* clubs. So I had to make one here for us to gather, to unite, and bring in people who like *forró*.

FIGURE 4.14 *Arlindo dos Oito Baixos (left), sanfona de oito baixos, and Biró, 120-bass accordion.* *(Photo by Megwen Loveless.)*

> I did this, and it has been a success. Here you'll find musicians, friends, people who like *forró*, Northeastern music, and the things of the North of Brazil. And I intend to keep it going.

Arlindo is quite clear on what styles are included in *forró pé-de-serra* and what the essential elements of its instrumentation are: "*Forró pé-de-serra* has the rhythms of *forró, baião, xote, chorinho, xaxado, arrasta-pé,* and *frevo.* What's important is that it be performed by *sanfona,* triangle, and *zabumba.*"

Arlindo's son Raminho, professional musician who accompanies his father on *zabumba,* describes the recent revival of interest in rootsy *forró* among young people:

> I think *forró* is roots music, original music. Since the time of Gonzaga's death, young people have rediscovered *forró. Forró* never died. Each year, after the St. John festivals, it declined a bit, but as soon as Carnaval was over, *forró* would return. But now it's different. Now *forró* is played all year long, and *forró pé-de-serra* is popular.

Sílvia Lúcia, a nonmusician who regularly attends Arlindo's Sunday night dances, describes the family environment and the friendly relations it encourages between musicians and audiences.

> Here it's a family environment. It's calm but at the same time we can have fun. Not to mention the artists who we meet here, their talent and their simplicity, which is the most important thing we see here. The simplicity of people who really know how to play. I also think it's beautful—and moving—to see people who really have talent speak with all of us like we're family. We feel at home here.

This is completely in keeping with the traditional hospitality of Northeast Brazilians, and is comparable to the emphasis on family ties that is highly valued in the *caipira* music culture of South Brazil.

Arlindo's identification with the accordion extends to his artistic name, which translates as Arlindo of the Eight Basses. "Basses" refers to the number of bass and chord buttons played by the left hand. This is not unusual for musicians in Brazil (or elsewhere). Heleno dos Oito Baixos, for example, from Caruaru, Pernambuco, became well known when his music was included in the recorded anthology *Brazil: Forró: Music for Maids and Taxi Drivers* (1989).

Arlindo was born on an *engenho* south of Recife and learned to play accordion by watching his father, who played for birthdays, weddings, and parties—not very well, but as Arlindo explains, "no lugar de cego quem tem olho é rei" (in the land of the blind the one-eyed man is king). Live music was highly valued in the countryside where he grew up. "To hear a radio playing was difficult," Arlindo remembers. "All you saw was sugarcane and forest. We learned the songs that people sang and whistled. Nobody talked about records." After the family moved to a larger town, Arlindo began playing for parties in place of his father. Later, moving to Recife and earning a living as a barber, he began working professionally in music after a radio station employee heard him playing during idle times at the barber shop. He then joined a band called Coruja e seus Tangarás, a *conjunto regional* whose members dressed in the manner of the famous bandit Lampião. He met Luiz Gonzaga when both their bands were playing at a fairgrounds in Recife, and Gonzaga invited him to join his band.

When Arlindo told Gonzaga that he wanted to make records of his own, Gonzaga advised him to switch to the *sanfona de oito baixos*, since there were fewer skilled players of that instrument, and he would have a better chance of standing out amidst the players of the 120-bass accordion who crowded the radio stations and recording studios. The 120-bass accordion uses the familiar design in which the right hand plays a piano-like keyboard and the left hand plays bass notes and chords on buttons. After three years of practice, Arlindo made a record deal with RCA with Gonzaga's help and began a recording career that continues to the present. He has also recorded for Polygram and Rozenblit, Recife-based label that distributed its records throughout Brazil in the 1950s–1970s.

In recent years Arlindo has had to cope with blindness caused by diabetes. Nevertheless, he has maintained an active schedule of performing, teaching, and recording, including two recent independent CDs, *Forró Pra 500 Anos* and *Dançando na Chuva*. The nationally famous accordionist and composer Dominguinhos said of Arlindo, "I think this artist of the eight-bass accordion is one of the best we have in the country."

The Technique of the Sanfona de Oito Baixos. The button accordion works differently from the piano accordion in a crucial way: on a piano accordion, the pitches on the keyboard remain the same while the bellows are opened and closed as needed. On a button accordion, each button produces two pitches from two sets of metal reeds. One is activated when the bellows are opened, the other when they are closed. (The harmonica, which produces different pitches when the player inhales and exhales, works on the same principle.) What this means for the button accordion player is that not only must the sequence of buttons be executed correctly, but the bellows direction must also be coordinated with the fingering. Moving the bellows in the wrong direction will produce a wrong note just as pressing the wrong button will. This different—and much more difficult—system means that the button accordion is not just a smaller accordion that the player of the 120-bass instrument can simply double on. It also means that despite its compact size, the button accordion is a complex instrument with a unique set of musical resources. Further information on the technique and tuning of this instrument may be found on the web site.

The Symbolic Importance of the Sanfona de Oito Baixos. Despite its difficulty, the *sanfona de oito baixos* symbolizes the rustic rural past for many *forró* listeners. Its nickname, *pé-de-bode*, translates as "goat's foot" and recalls the days when the instrument had only two basses; the analogy seems to be with the division of the goat's hoof into two parts. It is also called the *fole de oito baixos*—*fole* refers to the bellows.

This instrumental contrast is brought out in the well-known Luiz Gonzaga/Humberto Teixeira song "Respeita Januário." The song's narrator advises Gonzaga, whose father, Januário, played the *sanfona de oito baixos*, to respect his father's ability on the smaller instrument even though Gonzaga has achieved great fame by playing the 120-bass model.

Diego Reis, a young accordionist in Recife, described the instrument this way:

> Arlindo . . . specialized in this instrument called the *sanfona de oito baixos*, an extremely complicated instrument, difficult to play. Among musicians it's called the crazy person's instrument.

ACTIVITY 4.9 *Two versions of "Forró em Monteiro" by Arlindo dos Oito Baixos are included on the CD: an unaccompanied version recorded during a lesson (CD track 13) and a live recording from a Sunday evening* forró *party at Arlindo's house (CD track 14), during which this tune was played as part of a medley of instrumental* forró *tunes that lasted approximately twenty minutes. Listen to both versions as you follow these suggestions for listening.*

The Tune. The first half of the tune begins with a rising line that descends into busy figuration in a small range. This is repeated and ends with a triplet flourish that sounds more difficult than it is: all of the notes are played with closing bellows and they fit within one hand position, so no shifting is necessary. The second half of the tune is more contrapuntal. Further contrast is created by playing the repeat of the second half an octave lower. Photocopy the notation to write on it. Mark on the copy where the repetition of the first half of the tune occurs. Note the timing on the CD tracks where the second half of the tune begins and where it repeats. While the right-hand part creates three voices that are rhythmically offset, the left hand (heard most easily on the unaccompanied version) adds a fourth part which uses the basic *baião* rhythmic cell (see Figure 4.13). Listen for the slight variations in the left-hand part of the solo version.

FIGURE 4.15 *"Forró em Monteiro."*

Meter. The tune is felt in a quick duple meter. It is notated in 4/4 to facilitate reading. Listen to the solo version all the way through, following the notation, to be sure you are hearing the four-beat bars.

Bellows. "C" indicates notes played by closing the bellows, "O" by opening. Tunes composed on the *sanfona de oito baixos* tend to have groups of notes that use the same bellows direction. But quick changes of direction are also common, as in the second ending of the second half. The air accents produced by the bellows changes create another

FIGURE 4.16 Forró *percussion accompaniment.*

layer of rhythm. On the notation, bracket all the groups of notes played on one bellows push or pull. Then do those physical motions according to the groupings to feel the technique, and notice how rhythmic accents can be created by the bellows changes.

Rhythmic Accompaniment. Figure 4.16 shows the essential rhythmic accompaniment parts for you to follow; listen for one of them at a time all the way through. Two examples of the *zabumba* pattern are provided. As the live recording (CD track 14) shows, *zabumbeiros* improvise constantly to provide varied patterns of accents. The distinctive *forró* triangle pattern is produced by damping the first, second, and fourth sixteenths of each beat and letting the third one ring. This seemingly simple and repetitious part is very difficult to sustain during a long evening of playing for dancers at rapid tempos. The *pandeiro* part notated here is simplified. *Pandeiristas* in *forró* groups, however, create complicated patterns of accented sixteenth notes and are featured in solo breaks as well as in improvised solo breaks on *choro* standards such as "Escadaria."

FORRÓ AND NORTHEASTERN IDENTITY

Several elements combine to make *forró* a symbol of Northeastern identity. The strongest of these is Luiz Gonzaga: his music, his style of speaking and dressing, and his lifelong commitment to his native region. He continues to be a model for thousands of *forró* artists and for a large segment of the Northeastern musical public. Newly composed songs continue to use tropes of rural romance, nostalgic affection for the land, and hard luck that his songs established. Through its association with the June Catholic festivals, and all of the folkways that are associated with them, *forró* evokes in its listeners an idyllic rural image of bonfires, outdoor dances, straw hats and checkered shirts, and festive foods made with corn. In places like the Feira de São Cristovão, in Rio de Janeiro, where large numbers of Northeastern migrants gather for an open-air market on Sundays, *forró* is omnipresent.

In the early 2000s *forró* music and dance enjoyed a wave of national and even international popularity. It was very popular among young urban Brazilian audiences, especially college students in Rio de Janeiro and São Paulo. The band Falamansa had hit songs and appeared frequently on television. The group Mestre Ambrósio and the *forró* band led by singer Vanildo de Pombos performed in New York on the "Brazil: Beyond Bossa" program, part of the Lincoln Center Festival, in 2003. Mestre Ambrósio has toured the United States, Europe, and Japan. The band Forró in the Dark, led by U.S. accordionist Rob Curto (who has visited Arlindo's *forró*), performs regularly in New York clubs.

This chapter has presented three genres that serve as symbols of Northeastern identity. Performers of *cavalo-marinho* express popular Catholic devotion to the Three Kings, articulate an agricultural worker's vision of a moral order centered around patron–client relationships and the death and rebirth of a magical ox, and improvise songs full of local references accompanied by *rabeca* and *pandeiro*. While it is beginning to be performed elsewhere in Brazil and even in New York City, *maracatu* in both its varieties is strongly identified with Pernambuco. The deep drumming of the *maracatu de baque solto* recalls the coronation of Afro-Brazilian royalty, and the poetry, fast drumming, and multicolored costumes of *maracatu de baque virado* enchant the rural areas outside Recife with pageantry and mystery. While the first two genres preserve a local orientation, the *baião* and its associated style *forró* became national musics through the work of Luiz Gonzaga and countless musicians who worked in the style he established, including Arlindo dos Oito Baixos. Heartfelt songs of rural hardship accompanied by accordion, *zabumba*, and triangle can be heard all over Brazil, wherever Northeastern migrants have gone in search of better lives, but the sound always reminds listeners of the Northeastern backlands and the June patron saint festivals.

CHAPTER 5

Expressing Southern Brazilian Identity

The area of Southern Brazil to be discussed in this chapter includes the states of São Paulo, Minas Gerais, Goiás, and Rio Grande do Sul. While its population does include Brazilians of African and Brazilian Indian heritage, most of its residents are descended from Portuguese and other European immigrant groups, especially German, Italian, and Polish. The city of São Paulo, which at ten million people and a metropolitan area of more than fifteen million is the largest city in the region and in all of Latin America, includes among its residents a wide variety of Euro-Brazilian ethnic groups, a large contingent of Northeastern migrants and their descendants, many Brazilians of Middle Eastern descent, and a large Japanese-Brazilian community.

During the Christmas season, residents of Southern Brazilian small towns, and the big-city neighborhoods where lots of rural migrants live, reenact the journey of the Three Kings, the Magi, who seek the infant Jesus. People who represent the Three Kings go from house to house, stopping at the manger scene set up at each one, and sing traditional four-line verses in two-part vocal harmony to the accompaniment of the instruments that the Magi themselves are said to have played: *viola*, guitar with five double-coursed strings tuned to a triad; *caixa*, snare drum; and *pandeiro*. Such groups are called *Folias de Reis*, or "companies of kings" (Reily 2002). At secular dance events called *Catira* or *Cateretê*, a vocal duo, accompanied by *viola* and *violão*, sings long narrative songs called *modas-de-viola* that are punctuated by rhythmic instrumental interludes. These performances are part of *música caipira*.

Música sertaneja grew out of *música caipira* by modernizing its musical style while retaining its essential values. At the country's largest performance venues, on television specials, on FM radio, and on records that command a large share of the market, this kind of vocal duo sings songs full of romantic longing and nostalgia for rural ways, backed by guitars, bass, keyboards, and drums and sometimes by *rabeca*, accordion, steel guitar, and strings. The style of this music would strike a North American listener as almost identical to U.S. country music if not for the lyrics in Portuguese. And yet such vocal duos have a large and loyal public that does not consider them to be mere imitators, even when they perform their versions of U.S. country hits.

Música gaúcha is the music of the far southern states of Brazil, especially Rio Grande do Sul, which is part of a cultural area that also includes the *gaucho* culture of Argentina. It forms a distinct musical subculture within Southern Brazilian music. In this chapter I examine these three related styles that might sound "less Brazilian" to foreign listeners because they have been promoted abroad less often than *samba* and other genres with a strong Afro-Brazilian heritage.

MÚSICA CAIPIRA: RURAL MUSIC OF THE SOUTH

Música caipira is part of a rural way of life that owes much to the customs of the Portuguese settlers of Brazil and their descendants. *Caipira* technically refers to an inhabitant of the interior of São Paulo state and, by extension, to rural residents of South-Central Brazil. It also connotes cultural blending between Brazilians of Portuguese and Amerindian heritage, and, in some usages, has the pejorative sense of "hillbilly." The term *caipira* may be familiar to some readers from the piece by Heitor Villa-Lobos, "O trenzinho do Caipira" (The little train of the *Caipira*), from *Bachianas Brasileiras* No. 2.

Música caipira is distinguished by the prominence of vocal duos, usually male, who sing in thirds or sixths to the accompaniment of the *viola*. This tradition includes sacred music, including songs that are part of popular Catholic devotions such as the Folia de Reis, the Festa do Divino, and the dance for São Gonçalo, as well as secular music, including the Moda-de-Viola and Catira. Roberto Corrêa, the composer-performer-scholar whose music for *viola* is discussed below, extends the notion of *música caipira* to include new compositions that express the rural worldview and values, which he calls the *alma caipira*, or *caipira* soul (2000: 64). He does not mean that someone must be from a rural area to create it, or that everyone who is from a rural area can. It is a subtle quality, according to Corrêa, that can be perceived in the music.

ACTIVITY 5.1 *Locate the recording of "Vendi Minha Tropa (Paulista song)" from L.H.* Corrêa de Azevedo: Music of Ceará and Minas Gerais *(Rykodisc, 1997) on the CD itself or the short sample provided at amazon.com. Listen for the harmonization of the voices in thirds, the somewhat nasal vocal quality, and the accompaniment on the* viola, *which is both strummed during the sustained vocal passages and plucked along with the vocal line in more active vocal passages. Spoons provide extra rhythmic accompaniment. The title of this song means "I sold my herd." It was recorded in 1944 in Minas Gerais by Luiz Heitor Corrêa de Azevedo, a Brazilian musicologist. It is called a Paulista song because it uses the* caipira *style of São Paulo.*

Música Caipira *in a Sacred Context:* Folias de Reis. *Folias de Reis* (Companies of Kings) celebrate the Three Kings who sought the infant Jesus. The figures of the Kings visit houses to collect donations that will be used to finance the celebration that culminates the Christmas season: the *Dia de Reis,* or Epiphany, on January 6. They are accompanied by clowns who provide jokes, recite prophecies, and protect the group's banner. Beginning around December 24, the Company goes from house to house, stopping at the altar each one has set up, and offering a series of songs and recited texts on the theme of the Three Kings. Companies of Kings are active both in rural towns and in city neighborhoods with large populations of rural migrants.

Like *cavalo-marinho,* the Companies of Kings are one of many popular Catholic devotional practices that developed during the colonial era, when there were insufficient priests to serve the needs of the rural population. As a result, according to Reily, "Throughout much of the colony, religious life was left predominantly in the hands of laymen, who expressed their religious sentiments by drawing upon Portuguese forms of folk devotion, many rooted in late medieval musical practices" (2002: 7). Such devotions take the form of vows to a saint to perform a pilgrimage, an act of penance, or a performance in return for a blessing, such as the birth of a child or the curing of an illness.

The songs performed by Companies of Kings are called *toadas,* and their style corresponds to that of *caipira* music in general: vocal harmony, song texts in four-line stanzas, I-IV-V7 harmony, and accompaniment by *viola, pandeiro,* and *caixa*. In the Minas Gerais style of *toada,* a "little yell" on the syllable "ai" is added to the end of the stanza (Reily 2002: 35). This sample *toada* text comes from a prophecy recited by a *bastião* (clown) in front of a household manger scene.

E seguindo a santa estrela,	And following the holy star,
Os Três Reis são contentes,	The Three Holy Kings were happy,
Para ver nosso Jesus Menino,	To see our Baby Jesus,
Nosso Rei Onipotente.	Our Omnipotent King.

(Reily 2002: 146).

ACTIVITY 5.2 *If your university library owns* The Garland Encyclopedia of World Music, Volume 2: South America, Mexico, Central America, and the Caribbean, *or* The Garland Handbook of Latin American Music, *and the CDs that accompany them, listen to track 11 on the Garland CD, an example of music from* folias de reis *performed in São Paulo by a group from Minas Gerais. Listen for the way the accordion doubles the vocal melody and adds instrumental interludes; for the choral responses to the solo vocal melody; and for the rhythmic accompaniment on* pandeiro *that is less syncopated when compared with the use of* pandeiro *in* samba. *There are two high-quality recordings of music from* folia de reis *on the Villares and Vianna CD set* Música do Brasil, *cited in Chapter 1.*

In Reily's analysis, the heart of the ritual of the Companies of Kings is the reciprocal exchange of gifts, which begins with the story of the Magi: having brought gifts to the infant Jesus, they received musical instruments and were told to spread the good news. The Companies of Kings give music and blessings to those they visit in return for donations to support the January 6 celebration. This reciprocity is a fundamental value of caipira life. Participants in the Companies of Kings enact a Christian moral order that protects them from the effects of unequal power relations in both the rural world of landholders and tenant farmers and the urban industrial world of factory supervisors and workers.

Música Caipira ***in a Secular Context.*** One of the most important secular contexts for *caipira* music making is the *Catira,* a social dance also known as *Cateretê.* Two singers, one or both of whom play *viola,* stand at the head of two dancers and sing *modas-de-viola,* long narrative songs on themes of struggle, passion, life and death, daily life, or fantastic events. During the singing, the dancers keep still or add vocal responses. Between stanzas the *violeiros* play syncopated strumming patterns that are matched by the dancers' hand clapping and foot stamping.

Cantoria. Scholars have compared the *moda-de-viola* to medieval romances (epic tales), and it is considered the "most noble" of the *caipira* genres (Corrêa 2000: 71). It is also related to *cantoria,* a tradition of poetry and song with *viola* or guitar accompaniment that links the *sertão* of Central-Southern Brazil with that of the Northeast. This tradition includes *romances* (epic songs) and the *desafio* (song duel), in which each of two singers combines memorized rhymes and improvised lines in elaborate rhyme schemes in an effort to exhaust the other's memory and ingenuity. It flourishes both in the Northeast and in São Paulo, where it has a large audience among Northeastern migrants and others who are drawn to it. Kuarup Discos has released important recordings of *cantoria* featuring such artists as Elomar, Geraldo Azevedo, Vital Farias, and Xangai. *Cantoria* in turn is part of a tradition of verbal artistry that includes *literatura de cordel,* poetic works illustrated with woodcuts that are printed in small leaflets and sold in rural markets.

Música Caipira ***on Records and Radio.*** Broadcasting has played a major role in forming a national musical identity (see McCann 2004), a good example of which can be seen with *música caipira. Música caipira* began to attract national attention during the late 1920s, when Cornélio Pires made a series of 78-rpm recordings of it, at first independently and then on Columbia. Releases of *caipira* music followed on Odeon and Victor, and radio programs began featuring it around the same time. Record companies in many countries were also discovering that there was a market for regional and ethnic styles. During this same period, for example, Ralph Peer was recording the Carter Family of Virginia.

Pires's recordings and broadcasts helped to establish what became known as the "duo style": vocal duet in thirds and sixths; accompaniment by *viola* and guitar, which together became known as the "couple." The first voice is the higher of the two parts. Normally, the voices sound equal in strength, but in some duos one voice will project more strongly (Corrêa 2000: 70–1). Some composers added contrary or oblique motion in the voice parts or more elaborate harmonizations. A *sanfona* (accordion) can be added to the "couple" to provide harmonic support and improvise introductions and linking passages, which are called *costuras* (derived from the verb *costurar*, to sew) because they knit the sections together. The harmony is usually limited to tonic, subdominant, and dominant-seventh chords.

The form typically includes an introduction and single strophic section, sometimes with a refrain. The lyrics are in the form of *quadras* (four-line verses with seven syllables per line). Traditionally, songs could be extended as long as necessary—*modas-de-viola* had many verses. Performers had to shorten songs to fit within the 3–4 min. per side limit of the 78-rpm recording and the time limits of a radio program.

Like performers in many genres of Brazilian music, members of vocal duos chose artistic stage names. The *caipira* and later *sertaneja* duos carried this practice one step further by choosing names that are very similar, such as Tonico and Tinoco. When one partner died, left, or was replaced, the new one often used the same name or chose a similar one. I have heard Brazilians make fun of this custom, but Reily notes that there is a good explanation for it: metaphors drawn from family relationships are an important part of *caipira* musical discourse. Within the "couple" of *viola* and guitar, the former is considered the wife, the latter the husband. The vocal duos strive to be as close as brothers, both socially and musically, and so they name themselves the way many parents (not just in Brazil) name twins: with almost identical names, such as Waldir and Walmir or Leandro and Leonardo (Reily 1992: 346). Among the most significant *caipira* vocal duos are Zé Carreiro e Carreirinho, Tonico e Tinoco, Raul Torres e Florêncio, Tião Carreiro e Pardinho, and Pena Branca e Xavantinho.

Solo vocalists have also played a role in *caipira*. The most prominent among them is Inezita Barroso, who has had a distinguished career as an interpreter of a wide variety of Brazilian traditional and popular music, with special emphasis on *música caipira*. She is also an educator, actress, and radio and TV broadcaster. Since 1980 she has had a program on TV Cultura in São Paulo entitled "Viola, Minha Viola." In 2003, at 78 years of age, Barroso released her eightieth recording, *Hoje Lembrando*, on the eclectic label Trama.

ACTIVITY 5.3 *Use the links on the companion web site to listen to excerpts from Inezita Barroso's* Hoje Lembrando *on the Trama web site.*

In the 1960s, performers of *caipira* music began diversifying the genre to include music from other parts of Brazil (samba, *coco, embolada, baião*); the pan-Latin *bolero;* the Paraguayan *guarânia;* and the Mexican *corrido, canción ranchera,* and *huapango* (Reily 1992: 351; Corrêa 2000: 72–73). While most preserve the vocal duo format, these styles are distinguished by characteristic rhythms and instrumentation.

The Viola Caipira. The instrument most closely associated with *música caipira* is the *viola caipira,* a steel-string guitar with five pairs of strings. In Brazil the six-string acoustic guitar is called *violão,* and the electric guitar is called *guitarra elétrica* or simply *guitarra.* The *viola* was brought to Brazil by colonists from Portugal, where it was the instrument of troubadors. For centuries it was made by traditional craftsmen. In the early twentieth century, *violas* began to be mass-produced, including the *viola* with a metal resonator that is the favorite instrument of Northeastern players, who also use wooden instruments like those of Southern Brazil. Fine instruments are still made by luthiers today (Corrêa 2000: 21–4).

Dozens of *viola* tunings are in use in various regions of Brazil. All *violas* use five courses, or pairs of strings, with the two highest pairs tuned in unison and the three lowest tuned in octaves. The number of strings is usually ten, but some *violas* have twelve (two of the courses using three strings, as in the case of the *viola de Queluz*) and some fewer than ten and as few as five. A commonly used tuning is *Cebolão em Ré,* in which the three lowest pairs of strings sound at A2 and A3, D3 and D4, F♯3 and F♯4, and the two highest are in unison at A3 and D4 (using the pitch-naming system in which middle C is C4). In other words, the strings are tuned to a D major triad.

Traditional *violeiros* believe that the ability to play the *viola* is either a divine gift or something that a player must acquire by means of a *pacto-com-o-outro-lado* (a pact with the other side, or the Devil); they also put rattlesnake rattles inside the instrument to protect it (Corrêa 2000: 46, 53). A *violeiro* named Daniel, from Goiás, who was close to 100 years old at the time, told Corrêa:

> that he learned *viola* from an old man who had made the *pacto.* Daniel remembers that, once upon a time, this *violeiro* was playing for a dance and decided to join in the dance himself. He got up, rested the *viola* on the bench where he had been sitting, and entered the *roda* to *sambar* to the sound of his *viola,* which continued to play as it rested on the bench (2000: 51).

FIGURE 5.1 *Roberto Corrêa.* *(Photo courtesy of Roberto Corrêa.)*

Due to their prominent role in popular celebrations, *violeiros* have a distinguished position in their communities that can provoke either extreme humility or vanity.

Roberto Corrêa and the Viola Caipira. The best-known artist of the *viola caipira is* Roberto Corrêa (Figure 5.1). He learned to play acoustic guitar as a child and discovered the *viola* after moving to Brasília to study physics at the university. His intense interest in the *viola* has led Corrêa into a highly productive career. He has written a method for his instrument, entitled *A Arte de Pontear Viola* (The Art of Viola Playing, 2000). To distinguish *viola caipira* from the viola of the violin family and from other types of guitars, he prefers the term *viola de arame*: *arame* (wire) refers to the metal strings. He has recorded extensively and his CD *Viola Caipira—Brasil*, on the UNESCO-sponsored Traditional Music of the World label, is perhaps the easiest to find outside of Brazil. His solo recordings feature his *viola* playing and singing, and he has done many collaborative projects, including *Caipira de Fato*, his second CD with Inezita Barroso (1997), which won the Sharp Prize, the Brazilian equivalent of the Grammy. Corrêa has toured internationally and has taught *viola* at the School of Music in Brasília since 1985.

New compositions, whether modeled on traditional musical forms or not, are part of *caipira* music if they have the "*caipira* soul," says Corrêa. His compositions grow out of a lifelong attachment to *caipira* music, research on its origins and its practitioners, and intimate knowledge of the playing techniques and manufacture of his instrument.

ACTIVITY 5.4 *CD track 15 presents the composition, "Queluzindo," which was inspired by and performed on a vintage* viola *from Queluz (today called Conselheiro Lafaiete) in Minas Gerais, where there was an accomplished school of* viola *makers and players in the late nineteenth and early twentieth centuries. Listen for the way Roberto Corrêa's fingerpicking alternates between the melody on fretted and open upper strings and bass notes on open lower strings. Notice how the double-coursed strings create a natural phase shift effect: even though the* viola *is perfectly in tune, small differences in the pitch of strings tuned to a unison or an octave help to create the bright, ringing sound of this instrument. After you have noted the sound of the viola, shift your attention to details of the musical context. Listen for the themes and their repetition. For a more detailed listening guide, see the companion web site.*

MÚSICA SERTANEJA: BRAZILIAN "COUNTRY" MUSIC

Música sertaneja was one of the most popular Brazilian music genres in the 1980s and 1990s, and continues to be so at present. While it is performed and played on the radio throughout Brazil, it is especially popular among rural migrants to the large cities of Southern Brazil, especially São Paulo. *Sertaneja* originated and continues to be meaningful in the context of the large rural-to-urban migration since the 1930s that has transformed Brazilian society. It grew out of traditional music of the *caipira* vocal duos. According to Reily, "[t]he term *música sertaneja* became current only in the late 1950s, replacing the more pejorative term *música caipira*" (1998: 319). This is similar to the way "country" replaced "hillbilly" and "rhythm and blues" replaced "race" in the U.S. context.

Between the 1930s and the 1950s, duos such as Torres e Florêncio established an acoustic *sertaneja* sound: the vocal duet in thirds and sixths, with strummed guitar accompaniment and instrumental counterlines on a second guitar or accordion. The vocal style retained the nasal sound and rural diction of *caipira* style. Along with "Tristeza do Jeca," to be discussed below, the song "Chico Mineiro" (Tonico and Francisco Ribeiro) was popular during this period. The cowboy narrator laments the death of his *viola*-playing co-worker, who was shot during a visit to a festival, and discovers only after his death that they were really brothers (see Reily 1992: 349–50 for a transcription and translation).

In the 1960s, as migrants from rural areas and their descendants established urban lifestyles, the style of *sertaneja* became more "modernized" as the lyrics expressed more nostalgia for rural life. The modernization includes singing with more standard Portuguese pronunciation, fuller ensemble accompaniments, and the incorporation of solo vocal sections in the arrangements. The vocal duet continued to be a central element of the style. In arrangements by Leo Canhoto and Robertinho, for example, which had solo vocal sections, "[e]ach time the vocal duet was taken up, the audience would break into applause as it still does today, confirming the relational orientation of the migrants' ethos" (Reily 1992: 352). One of the first big hits in this style, according to Reily, was "Saudade da Minha Terra" (Nostalgia for My Land), by Belmont and Goiá, which begins

What good does it do me
To live in the city
If happiness
Doesn't come with me
Goodbye, Paulistinha

Of my heart
To my backlands
I want to return.

Today's *música sertaneja* preserves the traditional characteristics of singing in thirds, accompaniment by *viola* or acoustic guitar, songs in verse-chorus form, and song lyrics that evoke rural life and values or deal with love in sentimental terms. Its production values are very high, with elaborate arrangements including string sections, and vocal and instrumental parts with excellent intonation. The style of production is similar to that of country-and-western music produced in Nashville, including banjo picking, pedal steel guitar, a strong backbeat, and five- and six-string electric bass parts that carry the bass line into the extreme low register. Covers of U.S. country hits are common, but they are often new interpretations, with Brazilian cultural references, rather than just translations.

Zezé di Camargo e Luciano, brothers from Goiás, are one of Brazil's most popular *sertaneja* duos, along with Leandro e Leonardo and Chitãozinho e Xororó. Zezé first formed a duo with his brother Emival, who died in a car accident as they returned from a concert. He pursued a solo career and other collaborations before forming this duo with his younger brother Welson in 1991. Their first record sold 1.5 million copies; their 1998 CD sold 1.2 million copies *in anticipation of* its release. By their tenth anniversary, the duo had sold 17 million units. They have recorded soundtracks for popular *telenovelas* on Rede Globo, songs in Spanish, and a collaboration with Willie Nelson on "Always On My Mind." Their marketing emphasizes their rugged good looks and stylish clothes. The liner notes for their 2003 CD include twenty-two photos of the brothers, who also endorse a perfume called "Amor Selvagem" (Savage Love).

Zezé di Camargo e Luciano participated in the 2002 presidential campaign of Luiz Inácio "Lula" da Silva, which featured Zezé's song "Meu País" (My Country). This song occupies a middle position between "Aquarela do Brasil," which praises the country, especially Bahia, unquestioningly in stereotyped images, and the song also called "Meu País" by the hard-core rock band Devotos, discussed in Chapter 6, which juxtaposes national symbols such as Carnaval and soccer with the murder of street children. "Meu País" by Zezé di Camargo asks why, in a country so blessed by natural abundance ("where everything that's planted grows"), there should be a shortage of bread, and alludes vaguely to deceitful entities that are profiting from the labor of working people.

ACTIVITY 5.5 *Visit the web site for links to legal samples from CDs by Zezé di Camargo e Luciano. Compare the sound and studio production to that of traditional* música caipira.

The stylistic trajectory of *sertaneja,* however, has not been a simple movement from rustic *caipira* origins to slick Nashville modernity, and the significance of *sertaneja* for its audiences goes beyond nostalgia. Alex Dent argues that the revival of interest in caipira music and culture in general since 1985, when Brazil returned to democratic rule, can be viewed as a response to the increasingly impersonal nature of social life under neo-liberal economic conditions, which include privatization of state-owned companies and opening Brazilian markets to foreign investment and competition. Referring to the musical revivalists (who include Roberto Corrêa), Dent writes:

> Their musical practice focuses on the way in which democratization has not necessarily increased participation as promised, and in which liberalization has increased, rather than reduced, social disparities. All the while, an urbanization that began at the turn of the century but intensified in the late 1920s, Revivalists argue, has continued unchecked in its erasure of Brazil's rural traditions. In this way, Revivalists intervene in what they perceive to be a late twentieth century crisis. In sum, they use longstanding Central-Southern musical idioms in order to address what they portray as an imminent disappearance of tradition, and rectify an impending crisis of cultural reproduction that will result from an inability to express emotions appropriately (Dent 2003: 8).

This theme of intensified interest in the local as a response to late twentieth-century economic and cultural changes, including globalization, recalls the discussion of *maracatu* in the context of globalization in Chapter 4.

Música caipira, traditional music of the Central–Southern region, is distinguished by its use of vocal duos, the *viola,* sacred music that is performed during celebrations of popular Catholicism, and secular music that embodies a rural worldview. *Sertaneja,* a commercial popular music that developed from *música caipira,* retains the key *caipira* elements of vocal duos and accompaniment by string instruments and modernizes them with a fuller ensemble sound often modeled on U.S.

country music, more standard Portuguese prounciation, and lyrics that articulate the values of rural dwellers and their descendants who have migrated to large cities.

MÚSICA GAÚCHA: CELEBRATING BRAZIL'S FAR SOUTH

Just as the legacies of sugarcane cultivation and the slavery associated with it have shaped the culture of the Northeast region, the culture of the far South region of Brazil, especially the state of Rio Grande do Sul, has been shaped by cattle-raising and the values of its central figure, the *gaúcho* (cowboy). The *gaúcho* image connotes masculine independence. This is reflected in the musical style of *música gaúcha*, which refers to the music of South Brazil in general, as Reily explains:

> Only in the extreme South did the stereotype of the *gaúcho* (cowboy), androcentric and individualist, so influence the formation of the Lusitanian-Brazilian personality that parallel thirds and other polyphonic traits are less prevalent. There, male solos are far more common, and groups are more likely to sing in unison. Distinctively, the southern Brazilian states have received the musical legacy of waves of European immigrants, particularly Germans, who in isolated communities maintain their language and musical traditions (1998: 308).

Like *música caipira* and *música sertaneja*, música gaúcha is little known to listeners outside Brazil. Many readers will probably associate the Spanish term *gaucho* with the skilled horseman of the Pampas, the grasslands of Argentina and Uruguay, who was celebrated in the Argentine national epic, *Martín Fierro* (1872) by José Hernández.

Música Gaúcha and representations of Brazilian music in ethnomusicology. *Like filmmakers and editors of compilation CDs, scholars have a role in determining what sorts of Brazilian music will become better known outside of Brazil. My intent to include a section on* música gaúcha *in this book was strengthened by reading a review by Maria Elizabeth Lucas, an ethnomusicologist who studies southern Brazilian music, of* Brazilian Popular Music & Globalization *(Perrone*

and Dunn, eds., 2001), which includes an essay of mine on the band Mestre Ambrósio. Lucas argues that the book's emphasis on Tropicália, *Afro-Brazilian music from Salvador, and other Northeastern musics gives a distorted perspective on Brazilian popular music as a whole, which, given its title, the book aims to address (Lucas 2002). Elsewhere she argues for a new model for representation of Brazilian music that does not automatically give MPB a privileged position, but instead shows the diversity of regional styles that are being blended with global styles, a process she calls an example of "the 'traditionalization' of popular music and the 'popization' of traditional music" (2000: 44). Chapter 6 discusses further examples of these processes in the context of Recife's popular music scene.*

The Nativist Movement in Rio Grande do Sul. The *gaúcho* lifestyle became an important symbol of nostalgia beginning around 1900, when a modernizing economy and the growing power of the ranchers marginalized the real-life *gaúcho*. Social clubs were created to sustain *gaúcho* traditions, including music. In response to the increasing influence of U.S. culture after 1945, there was renewed interest in the clubs, and the first Center for Gaúcho Traditions was founded. The Gaúcho Traditionalist Movement was founded in the early 1960s to supervise the clubs, which now exist all over Brazil and in several other countries. The most recent phase of this effort is the nativist movement, which arose in the late 1970s as the centralizing power of the military government was declining and interest in regional culture was increasing throughout Brazil (Lucas 2000: 46–8).

The most important activity of the nativist movement is to organize festivals that last three or four days and attract between 2,000 and 15,000 people a day. Many of the participants wear traditional clothing: "baggy trousers embroidered at the sides (known as *bombachas*), a leather belt, leather boots with spurs, a triangular scarf worn around the neck over the shirt, and a hat" (Lucas 2000: 49). Versions of this clothing are worn by both of the artists to be discussed in this chapter, Leonardo (see Figure 5.3) and Renato Borghetti (see Figure 5.4). The festivals celebrate symbols of *gaúcho* life—including traditional music, drinking *maté* tea, and barbecues—that the educated middle classes would find coarse. Turning symbols that are put down by outsiders into symbols of pride is an important purpose of the festivals. This is similar to the celebration of *matuto* (hick) culture in the Northeast during the patron saint festivals in June, and to aspects of popular and youth culture in many places. Lucas explains the appeal of the festivals as follows:

> For the public in general, the great appeal of the nativist festivals is not the song competitions as such, but the social festive behaviour and interactions they promote within the sphere of play; they provide participants with the opportunity and the means to affirm a *gaúcho* identity, or, in other words, to reinforce the kind of sociability that is lacking in the patterns of interaction of modern urban life (2000: 49).

Traditionalist Música Gaúcha: *Leonardo.* The song competitions, however, are very important for songwriters, performers, and dancers. Song festivals make the musical goals of the nativist movement explicit by defining ideal types of song. In her study of the history of the festivals, Maria Elizabeth Lucas found a split between traditionalist composers, who celebrated the rural values of the region, and progressives, who incorporated urban musical references in their songs. Traditionalists tended to come from the pampa region, near Brazil's borders with Argentina and Uruguay, and their songs emphasize the natural beauty of the region and the values of rural life (Lucas 2000: 53). Their songs reflect a set of genres that are the product of the diffusion of salon dances in the later nineteenth century, including waltzes, polkas, and mazurkas. (Remember that the polka played an important role in the development of samba and *choro*.)

The song "Céu, Sol, Sul, Terra e Cor" is a *rancheira*, which grew out of the mazurka, and uses triple meter. In 2000 this song was chosen in a statewide newspaper poll as the song that best represents the *gaúcho* soul (Lucas 2000: 54), and audiences typically stand when it is performed. Its composer, Leonardo (Jader Moreci Teixeira) (Figure 5.2), was born in Bagé, Rio Grande do Sul, a small city near the border with Uruguay. His musical career has lasted forty years, with 800 recordings of his songs by himself and others, by his own estimation, and 41 records. He has won competitions at numerous song festivals and currently has a weekly program on Rádio Guaíba in Porto Alegre, the state capital.

FIGURE 5.2 *Leonardo.* *(Photo by Luiz Ávila.)*

ACTIVITY 5.6 *As you listen to CD track 16, an excerpt from "Céu, Sol, Sul, Terra e Cor" by Leonardo (Jader Moreci Teixeira), note the contrast between the lyrics of this song, which stress natural abundance ("where everything planted grows") and those of "Asa Branca," known as the "hymn of the Northeast," which speak of leaving the land because of drought. Use the elements of music (rhythm, melody, harmony, timbre) to frame a comparison between this song and a song from another region of Brazil. If you didn't know it was a Brazilian song, where might you guess it was from?*

Eu quero andar nas coxilhas	I want to walk on the grasslands
Sentindo as flechilhas das ervas do chão	Feeling the grass on the ground
Ter os pés roseteados de campo	To have my feet roughened from walking

Ficar mais trigueiro com o sol de verão
Fazer versos, cantando as belezas
Desta natureza sem par

E mostrar, para quem quiser ver
Um lugar pra viver sem chorar.

É o meu Rio Grande do Sul
Céu, sol, sul, terra e cor

Onde tudo que se planta cresce
E o que mais floresce é o amor.
Eu quero banhar nas fontes
E olhar horizontes com Deus
E sentir que as cantigas nativas
Continuam vivas para os filhos meus.
Ver os campos florindo e crianças sorrindo
Felizes a cantar
E mostrar, para quem quiser ver
Um lugar pra viver sem chorar.

in the country

Become browned by the summer sun
To write poetry that sings of the beauties
Of this unequaled nature

And show to whomever wants to see
A place to live without sadness
It's my Rio Grande do Sul
Sky, sun, south, land, and color
Where everything planted grows
And what flourishes most is love
I want to bathe in the springs
And see horizons with God
And feel that the native songs
Will be alive for my sons

To see the fields flowering and children
smiling
Singing happily

And show to whomever wants to see
A place to live without sadness

Renato Borghetti and Progressive Música Gaúcha. Composers of the progressive segment of the nativist movement address contemporary social issues and incorporate a cosmopolitan array of musical influences in their compositions.

FIGURE 5.3 *Renato Borghetti.* *(© Werner Maresch '05, www.alaskaaa.com)*

> Musicians such as the accordion player/composer Luis Carlos Borges as well as the button accordion player Renato Borghetti have managed to filter a diversity of musical idioms within the regional frame in such a way that their careers have reached international visibility (Lucas 2000: 55).

Renato Borghetti is a virtuoso player of the button accordion, called *gaita* in Rio Grande do Sul (Figure 5.3). He began his career by playing in competitions at festivals of the nativist movement and has gone on to release sixteen recordings and tour nationally and internationally.

I was able to hear Borghetti in concert in Rio de Janeiro in 2001 along with Zé Calixto, a master of the Northeastern button accordion style who lives in Rio de Janeiro. Two regional styles of the same instrument were represented because this was part of a series of concerts devoted to accordion styles throughout Brazil. Zé Calixto opened the concert with a program of *choros*. Renato Borghetti, who cut a dramatic figure with his long hair, wide-brimmed hat, boots, and billowing *bombacha* trousers, began his half of the concert with a duet with Zé Calixto that began with Luiz Gonzaga's "Assum Preto," a song in minor key whose melodic rhythms and contour are similar to those of "Asa Branca," and segued into "Milonga Para as Missões," a popuular instrumental dance tune. (CD track 17 and Activity 5.7) Later in his set, accompanied by guitar and flute/soprano sax, Borghetti did a full version of "Milonga Para as Missões." The two accordionists played together again on "Asa Branca." No one seemed to mind this repetition of repertoire.

The button accordion became popular in Rio Grande do Sul after 1875, when it was brought by Italian immigrants and displaced the *viola*. "The accordion was considered easier to learn and more suitable for the performance of the salon dance music that was reaching the rural folk" (Lucas 2000: 53n6).

The *milonga*, a traditional song type of Argentina and Uruguay, was an antecedent of the tango. It was known by this name circa 1850 and revived by traditionalist composers in the early twentieth century in pieces for voice and guitar. Its characteristic accompaniment rhythm, which is also found in the *tango* and *habanera*, is dotted-eighth, sixteenth, two eighths.

ACTIVITY 5.7 *As you listen to "Milonga Para as Missões" by Gilberto Monteiro (track 17), performed by Renato Borghetti, note the characateristics of the* milonga: *typically in a minor key, with tonic and dominant harmony, and melodies that start high and descend (Goyena 2000: 582–3). Starting at letter A, the harmony alternates between two bars of V7 (B7) and two bars of i (Emi). My transcription in Figure 5.4 is a simplified version of the melody that does not notate all of Borghetti's melodic ornamentations. The* milonga *rhythm can be heard in the accompaniment in the interlocking parts of the bass and drums. Use the elapsed time on the CD to mark the repetitions of the two main sections, marked A and B.*

FIGURE 5.4 *"Milonga Para as Missões."*

The CD from which "Milonga Para as Missões" is drawn has many other references to *gaúcho* culture. It is entitled *Gauderiando*, which comes from the adjective *gaudério*, which refers to traditional *gaúcho* culture and to merrymaking. Another song, "Prenda Minha" ("My *Prenda*"), uses the term for "the *gaúcho*'s female mate" (Lucas 2000: 57, 48). On another track, Borghetti is heard along with orchestral accompaniment playing a fantasia on the state anthem of Rio Grande do Sul, which was composed in 1838 by Joaquim José de Medanha. The CD closes with a suite of *gaúcha* dances performed by Borghetti and dancer Milton Mânica, whose steps are heard on the CD.

The Sound of the South. In recent decades, the requirements of festival competitions have become less restrictive, and the artistic debates over traditionalist vs. progressive positions have decreased in favor of a pluralistic approach. Song festivals are important because their formalized requirements make the musical markers of regional identity explicit and therefore open to debate. For example, songwriters are expected to use "authentic rhythms of Rio Grande" and to compose "songs representative of the authentic music of Rio Grande do Sul" (Lucas 2000: 55). Both traditionalists and progressives, however, share a desire to see more attention given to music from this region in the national music arena:

> [M]usicians, producers, music critics and audiences share a common feeling that the "sound of the South" (*o som do sul*) deserves a better position on the national scene. Rio Grande do Sul is recognized as the third largest market for record consumption and the second for record production in the country. Yet, for performers and composers who follow the *gaúcho* aesthetics as a way of constructing difference and of positioning and defining themselves against the hegemonic notions of what constitutes Brazilian music, there is currently no place in the national industry of stardom (Lucas 2000: 58).

In an effort to achieve such a place, a younger generation of performers has created a new style of dance music that has been called *tchê* music by journalists by analogy with *axé* music from Bahia. *Tchê* is a Southern Brazilian slang term used in conversation to refer to one's conversing partner and to indicate the speaker as *gaúcho/a* (as an English speaker would use "man").

Popular Music and Social Action in Porto Alegre. In this section I have concentrated on traditionalist music associated with the nativist movement in Rio Grande do Sul. It should also be pointed out that Porto Alegre also has a thriving modern popular scene that builds on the city's history as a center of *Jovem Guarda* enthusiasm and Beatlemania. The rock band Bidê ou Balde, for example, has gained national exposure. (Their CDs on the Rio Grande do Sul label Antídoto are distributed nationally by Abril Music.) The band Video Hits also made the transition from Porto Alegre to the national market but has since disbanded.

Porto Alegre is the site of World Social Forum, the yearly gathering that was founded in 2001 in opposition to the World Economic Forum in Davos, Switzerland (in 2004 it was held in India). Delegates call attention to the negative effects of globalization on poorer countries and the environment. Music is part of many official and recreational events at the forum, which draws over 100,000 people from nearly 100 countries. A news report just before the 2005 Forum stated that, "Held in and around a number of giant tents, the event takes on the atmosphere of an independent music festival, with lots of different traditional bands, dancers and singers to entertain delegates" (BBC 2005). The Forum's choral theme song, "Another World Is Possible," delivers the message over a reggae beat.

The music of Rio Grande do Sul, Brazil's southernmost state, presents some distinct differences from that of other regions of the country. Inspired by the symbol of the *gaúcho, música gaúcha* emphasizes solo song with European-style voice quality and vibrato, musical genres derived from European social dances, and lyrics that make reference to the land and the *gaúcho* lifestyle. The *gaita* (button accordion) is an important instrument in the region. The use of the genre *milonga* is a reminder of the proximity of this area to Argentina and Uruguay, with which it shares many musical characteristics. The festivals of the nativist movement are an important context for performing *música gaúcha*. Song competitions feature both traditionalist and progressive musical styles. Porto Alegre, the state capital, not only has a growing popular music scene but is also a center of municipal, national, and international progressive political activity.

The musicians, genres, and performance contexts discussed in Part II have provided a sample of the tremendous diversity of regional musics in Brazil: *capoeira* and the music of the Kayapó; *cavalo-marinho, maracatu* and *forró*; and *música caipira, sertaneja*, and *gaúcha*. In their vocal style, song texts, instruments, dance, and dress, musicians and audiences find signs of identity that link them to a region and to specific communities within that region. These regional ties take on added importance for people who must migrate to other parts of Brazil. Part III points out how musicians draw on regional musics as they interact with national and global styles.

CHAPTER 6

The Innovative Music Scene of Recife

BRAZILIAN MUSIC AND COSMOPOLITANISM

Brazilian musicians demonstrate cosmopolitanism by participating in genres that can be considered global and by sharing Brazilian genres with the world. For the purposes of this chapter I'll use the term "cosmopolitan" to mean being aware of and participating in global flows of music and ideas, and having a worldview that includes the local and global and the many connections between them. This is by no means a recent development; the development of *bossa nova* is just one example of a previous cosmopolitan movement within Brazilian popular music. However, the rapid expansion of communications networks over the past fifteen years, a feature of globalization, has intensified the circulation of musical styles and presented local musical communities worldwide with new challenges, opportunities, and pressures. In retrospect, it seems logical that Recife would be the scene of productive interaction among musicians who practice local and global styles. As previous chapters have shown, many thriving traditional genres are found there and in surrounding areas of Pernambuco state. The generation of Recife young people who absorbed them while growing up in the 1980s and 1990s also had access to a wide variety of popular music from elsewhere. This chapter presents a sampling of their creative projects, which use the languages of rock, rap, and electronic music in distinctively Brazilian ways.

I have focused on the Recife scene because it has attracted national and international attention as a creative center since the mid-1990s, and because it is the popular music scene that I have direct experience with. Before getting into that discussion, however, I would like to suggest just a few cosmopolitan artists who are nationally and internationally prominent so that readers can investigate their work. If this book could have been longer, I would have devoted entire sections to these artists and many more.

Cássia Eller. Cássia Eller was a rock singer whom journalists called the most important pop/rock vocalist of the 1990s, and her last CD, *Acústico* (in the Brazilian MTV Unplugged series), sold hundreds of thousands of copies. Her preceding CD, *Com Você . . . Meu Mundo Ficaria Completo* (With You. . . . My World Would Be Complete), was very successful as well, and includes songs by Nando Reis, Carlinhos Brown, Caetano Veloso, Marisa Monte, and Gilberto Gil. She also had special affection for songs by the Beatles. She sparked controversy by being openly lesbian (she and her partner were raising a son, who was eight at the time of her death), wearing a mohawk, and appearing partially nude on television. When she died at 39 in December 2001, her career was at its peak.

Tribalistas. This 2003 CD is a collaboration by three of the most accomplished artists in current Brazilian music: Arnaldo Antunes, vocalist with the São Paulo rock band Titãs (Titans); Carlinhos Brown, the composer, vocalist, and multi-instrumentalist from Salvador, Bahia; and Marisa Monte, the vocalist, guitarist, and composer, whose many recording projects have included nearly every genre of Brazilian music and many international collaborators. The songs on *Tribalistas* are mostly love songs—the title track vaguely defines an "anti-movement" called tribalism. The vocal blend and the extremely well-crafted arrangements repay repeated listening. Brown, especially, plays a large number of instruments. The liner notes include English translations and chord symbols.

Hermeto Pascoal. Hermeto Pascoal, born in rural Alagoas in 1936, is a prolific composer and multi-instrumentalist. Widely regarded as a genius, a wizard of sound making, and one of the most musical individuals on the planet, he gained international prominence in 1970 when he recorded with Miles Davis. Pascoal's music is rooted in the musical traditions of his native Northeast, including *frevo* and *baião*, but he considers his music to be universal. He is also well known for playing multiple instruments and for producing musical sounds from everyday objects such as a tea kettle. In such recordings as *A Música Livre de Hermeto Pascoal* (1973), *Slaves Mass* (1977), *Zabumbê-Bum-Á* (1979), *Cérebro Magnético* (1980), *Só Não Toca Quem Não Quer* (1987), and *Mundo Verde Esperança* (2003), Pascoal and his collaborators have created music that clearly earns the label *sem rótulo*, or as Duke Ellington would put it, "beyond category."

FIGURE 6.1 *Central Recife; part of old Recife is visible at left.* *(Photo by Eduardo Queiroga, Agência Lumiar de Fotografia, www.lumiarfoto.com.br.)*

THE *MANGUE* MOVEMENT, CHICO SCIENCE & NAÇÃO ZUMBI, AND POPULAR MUSIC IN RECIFE

In 1990, a study of 100 of the world's major cities in terms of quality of living conditions ranked Recife among the five least livable (Anderson 1990). While the crime rate, transportation, and city services were indeed problematic, the study did not include richness of musical traditions in its data. In the city and in surrounding rural areas, musical traditions such as *cavalo-marinho* and *maracatu* were very strongly maintained, even though public awareness of them was much lower than it is today.

Since the mid-1980s, young musicians, journalists, and artists had been finding each other and discovering shared interests: in punk, funk, and hip-hop as well as *maracatu* and *coco*, and in James Brown and Afrika Bambaataa as well as Luiz Gonzaga and Jorge Ben Jor. In the early 1990s, an idea grew out of this circle of friends for a movement called *mangue*, after the fertile tidal mangrove swamps that lined the waterways of central Recife, where the Capibaribe and Beberibe Rivers meet the Atlantic Ocean (Fig. 6.1). This rich ecosystem is also where some of the poorest people in Recife live, in precarious houses built over the mud.

FIGURE 6.2 *Chico Science & Nação Zumbi. (L to R) Guest artist Gilberto Gil, Chico Science, Pupilo, Canhoto.* *(Photo by Geyson Magno, Agência Lumiar de Fotografia, www.lumiarfoto.com.br.)*

The *mangue* movement's two most important bands are Chico Science & Nação Zumbi (Figure 6.2) and Mundo Livre S/A. Chico Science was the artistic name of Francisco França, the highly charismatic lead vocalist of the band Nação Zumbi (Zumbi Nation), who died in 1997 at age 30, at the peak of his fame, in a car accident during Carnaval season on the highway between Recife and Olinda. The "Zumbi" in the band's name is the same Zumbi as the one sung about in the *capoeira ladainha* discussed in Chapter 3. The band had released the CD *Afrociberdelia* the year before, which followed their highly successful debut 1994 CD *da lama ao caos*, both on Sony. *CSNZ*, a double CD of studio tracks, live recordings, and remixes, was released after Chico Science's death.

Nação Zumbi has continued to be active, with Jorge dü Peixe assuming the lead vocal role as well as playing percussion. The rest of the band includes Lúcio Maia, guitar; Dengue, bass; Gilmar Bolla 8, percussion and vocal; Toca Ogan, percussion and voice; and Pupilo, drums and percussion. The band released the CD *Rádio S.AMB.A* on the YBrasil? label in 2000 and *Nação Zumbi* and *Futura* on the Trama label in 2002 and 2005, respectively.

The music of Chico Science & Nação Zumbi (CSNZ for short) and Nação Zumbi (NZ) is striking on many levels, starting with the rhythmic feel. Syncopated patterns played on three *alfaias* (the large, deep drums of *maracatu de baque virado*), electric bass, and bass drum create a heavy bottom end, over which are layered accented sixteenth-note subdivisions on the snare; *berimbau*, *reco-reco*, *agogô*, and smaller hand drums; and on some tracks, turntable scratching. Vocals by Chico Science, and to varying degrees by other members of the band, occupy a fascinating middle ground between rhythmic spoken words and singing. One might be tempted to call it a mixture of rap with Northeast Brazilian *embolada* (rapid improvised poetry over a *pandeiro* accompaniment), but the sound is so original that simply labeling it a mixture does not do justice to the band's transformation of those two genres and a variety of others. In the liner notes to *CSNZ*, Jorge dü Peixe called attention to the multiple styles the band draws on:

> There's nothing wrong with combining Grand Master Flash with Cajú e Castanha. Kraftwerk and *côco de roda*. Virtual beats that lead us to the *côco*. *Maracatu*, *ciranda*, soul, calypso, makossa, funk and *samba*.

Woven through this already powerful mixture of strong rhythms in all registers and vocals that are sometimes tuneful and sometimes not, but always strongly rhythmic, is Lúcio Maia's electric guitar work, which covers styles that range from choked-string rhythm parts to ringing Afropop sounds to rapid-fire thrash-metal chords to surf guitar to distorted heavy metal leads. The combination of drum set, *alfaias*, and Maia's guitar sound is extremely powerful. Critic Ben Ratliff, in a review of NZ's performance at the Abril Pro Rock festival in Recife in 2001, wrote that "[w]ith the growing interest in Latin American rock, Nação Zumbi might be one of the greatest rock bands in the world" (2001).

One of the aspects of CSNZ's music that Brazilian listeners find so compelling, but is naturally more difficult for non-Portuguese speakers to appreciate, is the band's lyrics, which are streetwise, slangy, and rooted in the neighborhoods of Recife on the one hand but universal in their depiction of urban experience on the other. On *da lama ao caos*, for example, the song "Rios, Pontes & Overdrives" (Rivers, Bridges & Overpasses) names Recife neighborhoods, while the song "A Cidade" (The City) tells of a city that never stops growing, with a widening gap between rich and poor. Jorge dü Peixe explained in a 2001 interview that he likes to write lyrics that are not tied to a specific time or issue: "This desire to be atemporal, to not be restricted to a single limited time, is something I'm concerned with." A generalized sense of nostalgia is a prominent theme of the lyrics on *Rádio S.amb.A*; Jorge suggested the song "O Carimbó/Côco Assassins" as an example. Evoking a sense of place is another. "I like landscapes and images a lot," Jorge said.

ACTIVITY 6.1 *Use the links in the Resources section and on the companion web site to listen to "Rios, Pontes, & Overdrives" at the Luaka Bop web site, and samples of Nação Zumbi's music and video at the Trama web site. Listen for the style features described above.*

Jorge dü Peixe and Lúcio Maia (Fig. 6.3) reflected in that 2001 interview on the aftermath of Chico Science's death in 1997. Chico, they said, wanted to change Recife for the better to make a better life for himself and his children. People wanted to make him into a saint after his death, but to them he was a good friend and a regular guy. The capsule sum-

FIGURE 6.3 *Nação Zumbi. (L to R) Gilmar Bolla 8, Jorge dü Peixe, Toca Ogan, Lúcio Maia. (Photo by Geyson Magno, Agência Lumiar de Fotografia, www.lumiarfoto.com.br.)*

maries of the *mangue* movement (including my own) tend to make it sound very self-conscious. But they formed the band not out of a calculated sense of what they should do but according to their own creativity with a *faça você mesmo* (do-it-yourself) spirit.

They also talked about the issue that was prominent in nearly every conversation I had in 2000 and 2001 with musicians who were part of the alternative music scene: the difficulty of getting radio airplay and the consequences that follow from that. Lúcio Maia said:

> If you don't get radio airplay, it's difficult to book concerts. You can't get into the market and it makes it more difficult to do other things that derive from that. [. . .] We don't wait for the radio stations [to play our music]. It's a complicated and very difficult situation. This is why Nação Zumbi has not managed to achieve the top level of success in Brazil. At the same time, in Europe and the United States, we are always hearing people say, "how come you don't get radio airplay? why aren't you a huge success?"

My interviews with radio program directors, market researchers, and a wide range of people involved in the Recife music scene in 2000–2001 showed that access to the media is the key issue for musicians in the local alternative scene, and independent labels have difficulty getting their music played because, even though some program directors deny it, others confirm that the big labels pay for airplay, sometimes directly (which is illegal in Brazil), other times indirectly (which is legal) in the form of merchandise offered to the stations to use in promotional giveaways. The practice of paying for airplay, known as payola in the United States, is called *jabá* in Brazil. Jorge dü Peixe and Lúcio Maia had strong feelings on this topic. In Maia's words,

> In Brazil, people are manipulated by the mass media, like TV and radio, so you can't say that this [low-quality popular music; the example they gave is music with repetitive nonsense refrains] is what people want. They impose it on people by playing it so much that people end up wanting to hear it. So it's obvious that people will request it. If they had the courage to play good music, not just the music of the new Recife scene, but good music from all over the world, all of this would change. It's not the people's fault. It's *their* fault.

Many people in the Recife metropolitan area, especially those who live in peripheral suburbs, cannot afford to buy CDs frequently, so they depend on radio, TV, and free public performances. Nação Zumbi and

Mundo Livre S/A have collaborated with the state government to offer the *Acorda Povo* project, a series of performances and workshops in such neighborhoods, which has taken place for several years running. Each performance pairs a well-known band, such as Nação Zumbi, Mundo Livre S/A, Mestre Ambrósio, Devotos, Faces do Subúrbio, or Sheik Tosado, with a local band from that neighborhood, both of which get paid, and is preceded by workshops on music and other arts. The enthusiastic responses from audiences show that the public taste is much broader than what is represented by FM radio playlists.

One episode that occurred early in my research in 2000–2001 demonstrated the power of the record companies and CD marketers to shape musical categories and marginalize the extremely varied and creative popular music produced by Recife's alternative scene. The manager of a downtown record store had agreed to provide me with a list of the top-selling CDs from the previous month. Since some of the artists on the list were unfamiliar to me, he agreed to list the style of each one. In order of most to least sales, the categories were *MPB, pagode, brega,* rock *nacional, forró, pop nacional, regional, axé, sertaneja, pop internacional,* and so on. When we came to Chico Science & Nação Zumbi, he put the band in the "regional" category, along with the noted *repentista* (singer of improvised verses or *repente*) and *violeiro* (guitarist) Ivanildo Vila Nova and the *embolada* duo Caju and Castanha. In 2002, the airplay situation improved somewhat through a government-sponsored project to create several radio shows with local content.

The point of this discussion of radio airplay and categorization is that certain musical styles can become strongly associated with a region of Brazil, and this is generally a good thing: a source of pride, a tradition that young musicians can learn and then modify, a focus of tourism. But it can also become unhelpful when musicians from those regions who make music that doesn't fit the regional stereotypes are denied opportunities for recording, airplay, or touring. The innovative musicians described in this chapter would not deny the importance of regional musical styles. They do, however, criticize the way such regional preconceptions create barriers to their entry into the music market.

MUNDO LIVRE S/A: WORKING TOWARD A FREE WORLD

Mundo Livre S/A (hereafter MLSA) is one of the principal bands of the *mangue* movement. Like CSNZ's *da lama ao caos*, MLSA's 1994 CD *Samba*

Esquema Noise is a definitive statement of the new sound from Recife. The first track, "Manguebit," mixes biological and technological images by comparing the narrator to a transistor, Recife to a circuit, and Brazil to a chip. When the Recife scene started getting attention in the press, some journalists described it with the phrase "manguebeat" (which sounds the same as "manguebit" in Portuguese), which implied that there was a single beat or rhythmic feel that defined the new style. This isn't the case; the *mangue* concept is an aesthetic that embraces a wide variety of musical styles and emphasizes artistic intervention in the cultural life of the city.

Mundo Livre S/A was founded by Fred Montenegro, who uses the artistic name Fred04 (after the last two numbers on his government ID card; in conversation he is sometimes referred to as "zero quatro"), his brother Fábio, and two friends in 1984. The name of the band, which translates as "Free World, Inc.," is a reference to the TV series "Get Smart" (1965–70), in which the hapless spy Maxwell Smart is reassured by his boss, "It's all for the good of the free world"; it can also be interpreted as both a reference to the Cold War in general and to progressive political movements past and present. After Fred04 spent time in São Paulo in the late 1980s, he reformed the band (Figure 6.4) with his brothers, Fábio (bass) and Tony (drums), and Bactéria (keyboards) and Otto (percussion).

Fred04 was inspired to take up *cavaquinho* and guitar and to begin writing songs by the soul- and rock-influenced sambas on the Jorge Ben Jor (then Jorge Ben) album *A Tábua de Esmeralda* (Teles 2000: 272). The title of the band's first CD pays homage to Ben Jor's *Samba Esquema Novo* (1963). Fred04 was trained as a journalist, worked in radio in Recife, and is outspoken on issues of popular music, the media, and politics. The band's repertoire ranges from carefree love songs, such as "Meu esquema," which was used as the theme of the series "Tudo de Bom" on MTV Brasil, to songs about corporate domination of cultural life, such as "Batedores," both from the CD *Por pouco*. Fred04 joins a long tradition of Brazilian songwriters who have used popular song to address cultural, social, and political issues. He is also not afraid to include spoken discourses on matters that concern him in the band's shows.

Mundo Livre S/A has released five CDs: *Samba Esquema Noise* (1994), *Guentando a ôia* (1996), *Carnaval na obra* (1998), *Por pouco* (2000), and *O Outro Mundo de Manuela Rosário* (2003). In 2004, the band released *BIT*, a boxed set containing the band's first four CDs and a DVD with ten video clips on the Deckdiscs label.

FIGURE 6.4 *Fred04 of Mundo Livre S/A.* (*Photo by Fábio Braga.*)

While all of Mundo Livre S/A's CDs and live shows have an activist edge, "O Outro Mundo de Xicão Xukuru" is perhaps their most direct and outspoken song. It tells the story of the assassination of a leader of the Xukuru Indian community in western Pernambuco state near the city of Pesqueira. The case of the Xukuru Indians is a reminder that there are Brazilian Indian peoples still living outside of the Amazon region and still in conflict with surrounding Brazilian cities and governments and the Catholic Church. It highlights struggles over land and power, and it shows intellectuals, in this case Fred04 and the band, using their access to communications media to raise awareness of a pressing indigenous issue through music. This engagement in social issues is typical of musicians in the Recife alternative scene.

The Xukuru of Pernambuco are among those indigenous groups that were believed to have disappeared or blended into the general Brazilian population through (sometimes forced) intermarriage. In recent decades they have returned to public prominence and struggled to retain control over their lands. They presently number approximately 8,500 and live on 70,000 acres in western Pernambuco. Xicão, who led the Xukuru for approximately twelve years, was assassinated on May 20, 1998. Marcos de Araújo, the son of Xicão, is the new leader. The Xukuru were mentioned for the first time in Portuguese sources around 1700. Their first contacts with Portuguese settlers were violent. After their defeat they were settled in missionary villages and encouraged to intermarry with members of other indigenous groups and the Brazilian population. They have resisted a long series of efforts, both legal and extralegal, to appropriate their land and suppress their culture. In recent years their cause has been aided by anthropologists and religious groups, including the Conselho Indigenista Missionário (Missionary Indigenous Council, or CIMI) (Rabben 2004: 153–55).

Fred04 learned the story of Xicão in a documentary made by TV Viva, a socially engaged video production studio in Olinda, near Recife. As a young man, Xicão traveled to São Paulo, worked as a laborer, and played drums in a rock band. When he was struck by a mysterious illness, he returned to the Xukuru community, where an indigenous healer explained to him that he was destined to be the leader of the community and would only return to good health if he stayed there. He accepted the responsibility and led his people in struggles over land with neighboring large landholders. Fred04 also found it significant that Xicão's given name was Francisco de Assis (which would be Francis of Assisi in English), like that of Chico Science (Donato, n.d.).

ACTIVITY 6.2 *As you listen to CD track 18, "O Outro Mundo de Xicão Xukuru" by Mundo Livre S/A, focus on the mixture of samba elements (*cavaquinho *and percussion), rock drum and guitar parts, and a flute part that makes reference to indigenous music and follow the lyrics.*

[spoken by Fred04]

Numa faixa de terra de 28,000 hectares, localizada no agreste pernambucano, habitam cerca de 8,000 seres da espécie humano.	In a strip of land measuring 28,000 hectares, located in the *agreste* of Pernambuco [a transitional zone between fertile coastal area and dry

	interior area], live close to 8,000 beings of the human species.
[sung by Fred04]	
Eles não querem vingança	They don't want vengeance
Eles só querem justiça	They just want justice
Querem punição	They want punishment
Para os covardes assassinos	For the cowardly assassins
De seu bravo cacique Xicão	Of their brave Chief Xicão
[sung by Jorge dü Peixe (of NZ, a guest on the recording)]	
Eles não querem vingança	They don't want vengeance
Eles só querem justiça	They just want justice
[spoken by Fred04]	
Distribuídos por 23 aldeias, permanecem resistindo após quase quinhentos anos de massacres e perseguições, reivindicando nada menos que o reconhecimento e a demarcação da terra sagrada que herdaram de seus ancestrais.	Distributed in 23 villages, they have resisted massacres and persecutions for almost 500 years, demanding nothing less than the recognition and demaraction of the sacred land that they inherited from their ancestors.
[sung by Fred04]	
Ele não vai ser enterrado	He will not be buried
Ele não vai ser sepultado	He will not be entombed
Ele vai ser plantado	He will be planted
Para que dele nasçam novos direitos	So that new rights can grow from him

See the companion web site for the remainder of the lyrics.

The music business emerged as a prominent topic in my conversations with Fred04 in 2001, just as it had with Jorge dü Peixe and Lúcio Maia. In this case it was a question of CD distribution more than radio airplay. At a time when "Meu esquema" from the CD *Por pouco,* a romantic song in *bossa nova* style that was MLSA's first national hit, was being played often on MTV and on FM radio throughout Brazil, including Recife, the CD was not to be found in stores, since the first shipment sold out quickly and wasn't replaced. Fred04 locates the problem in the lack of connection between what is getting radio airplay (on three of the biggest FM stations, in the case of "Meu esquema") and what is being requested in stores, on the one hand, and what is supplied by the principal CD distributor, based in Recife, which controls a chain of stores and supplies the large supermarkets where many CDs are sold throughout the Northeast, on the other.

Fred04 also addressed the prejudice on the part of music industry executives that limits the entry into the national music scene of bands from Recife and the Northeast that don't play *forró* or other genres traditionally associated with the Northeast.

> There's that strange thing that gets repeated, which has even resulted in newspaper articles here in Recife, "this *mangue* scene has really made news all over the world, and has international prestige, but in commercial terms, it hasn't established itself, it doesn't make a commercial sound, it doesn't make a commercially viable sound." First of all, there is no one single *mangue* sound. You have Mestre Ambrósio and you have Devotos. Every style in the national pop market that you can imagine today in Brazil is played in Recife. What is so complicated in the sound format and the sonority of Devotos, for example, compared to that of Raimundos? How is it that Devotos are too complicated and Raimundos aren't? It's prejudice.
>
> Author: What kind of prejudice?
>
> Fred04: Prejudice of the radios.
>
> Author: Against . . . ?
>
> Fred04: Against pop music that comes from the Northeast. It has become a convention that a punk rock band has to be from São Paulo, or from Rio, or from Brasília. The Northeast, in the mind of some radio programming directors in São Paulo and Rio, which is the showcase of Brazil, in the mind of someone who is a distributor, the guy that puts the CDs in the stores, for him, a band from Recife has to play *forró, baião,* I don't know what. There's a prejudice that for a band to be successful outside of Recife it can't play an advanced, cosmopolitan, urban sound. Recife is treated traditionally by the media, principally by the market and the distribution networks, as a supplier of regional, traditional music, preferably with a rural accent.

Fred04 continues to link cultural production to the wider world of politics and economics. In a short article that accompanies a boxed set of MLSA's CDs, Fred04 makes references to the war in Iraq and the death there in 2003 of the United Nations High Commissioner for Human Rights, the Brazilian Sérgio Vieira de Mello; to NAFTA (the North American Free Trade Agreement); to Subcomandante Marcos, the leader of the Zapatista Army of National Liberation in Chiapas, Mexico; to online music file-sharing; to the radio airplay situation in the Northeast discussed above; and to the good news that Recife has more of a recording industry than it had ten years ago. And he cites Chico Science and the utopian vision of the *mangue* movement, and reflects:

> In the final analysis, to come and go, to keep moving, crossing borders, letting information (bits) flow; more than mere slogans, they have been—and continue to be—fundamental concepts for the collective utopia of manguetown . . . (2004)

This discussion of media politics is directly related to the themes of this book. It is one thing for scholars to argue that certain musical styles articulate national identity, regional identity, and cosmopolitanism. It is another to ask how audiences get access to that music, and how the conditions of their access to it shape the message. For example, the use of Northeastern traditional music in a film or a *telenovela* that perpetuates outdated stereotypes of people from the Northeast will have a very different impact from that of the performance of Northeastern traditional music at one of Recife's festivals, which also feature collaborations between traditional musicians and musicians with a cosmopolitan approach. The former kind of exposure reaches a much larger audience. And if the playlist of an FM station that claims to play the best of national and international popular music ignores local music that is just as carefully crafted, and just as well produced and recorded, that sends the message that the local music doesn't matter as much.

DEVOTOS: A HARDCORE LOOK AT LIFE IN RECIFE

The band Devotos (Figure 6.5) was formed in 1988 by vocalist and bassist Cannibal (Marconi de Souza Santos), guitarist Neilton, and drummer Celo Brown under the name Devotos do Ódio (Devotees of Hate), which was borrowed from the title of a book by José Louzeiro (1987) (Teles 2000: 244). Louzeiro is the novelist, journalist, and screenwriter whose *Infância dos Mortos* (Childhood of the Dead), a book about the life of a street child that was made into the critically acclaimed 1981

FIGURE 6.5 *Devotos. Cannibal (foreground), Neilton (back left), Celo Brown. (Photo by Geyson Magno, Agência Lumiar de Fotografia, www.lumiarfoto.com.br.)*

film *Pixote* by Hector Babenco. The group was and still is based in the Alto José do Pinho neighborhood of Recife, a low-income hillside neighborhood that has both abundant social problems and many people working to improve conditions there. They changed the name of the band to Devotos in 2000.

When MTV began to be broadcast in Recife (over the airwaves, not on cable), the signal could be picked up clearly in the Alto José do Pinho neighborhood, and the future members of Devotos listened to punk rock and bands like The Smiths and The Cure along with punk rock from São Paulo. They were aware of the traditional genres that Chico Science & Nação Zumbi and other bands would later incorporate into their sounds, but they were interested in playing a melodic style of hardcore rock (Teles 2000: 248).

The members of Devotos embrace the do-it-yourself ethic of punk rock. Guitarist Neilton explained to me in 2001 how he made his first guitar and amplifier himself—including carving the fingerboard and body of the guitar and winding the coils of the pickups—and played it for a long time without anyone noticing that it wasn't store-bought. Neilton's creativity extends to the artwork on the bands' CDs and the design of their web site. In addition, band makes its own instrument cases and speaker cabinets, only buying what they can't make themselves. This isn't done, however, with a sense of deprivation. On the contrary, Neilton says, "I don't feel anguish about it. I take pleasure and pride in having done it, and having my work out there, a simple pride in seeing my work done . . . the idea conceived."

Neilton was able to buy Gibson and Fender guitars and a Marshall amplifier once the band became more successful, but he still felt the need to play with people's perceptions of product labels. He bought a cheap electric guitar, removed everything, including frets, made it over in his style, gave it the brand name "Robson," and started using it in concerts. Soon people were admiring its sound and asking where they could buy one.

Among the obstacles the band faced in its early years were police repression and the disapproval of neighborhood residents for their choice of musical style. The Alto José do Pinho was home to *caboclinhos* and *maracatu* groups that were prominent during Carnaval. The media image of rock bands linked them to middle-class youth. When Devotos began getting press coverage, it was due in part to the perceived incongruity of a group of lower-class youths playing hardcore rock (Teles 2000: 251). Over time the band's relationship to the community improved, as it demonstrated its commitment by attracting abundant press attention to the many bands that had formed there, and founding a non-governmental organization, Alto Falante (a play on the literal expression "loudspeaker," *altofalante*, and the name of the neighborhood, "Alto," speaking, or "falante"), which does cultural and social projects.

The band has released three CDs: *Agora tá Valendo* (BMG, 1998), *Devotos* (Rockit!, 2000), and *Hora da Batalha* (independent, 2004). To return to the theme of Brazilian national identity that is addressed in such songs as "Aquarela do Brasil," by Ari Barroso, listen to "O Meu País" (My Country) from *Devotos* as an example of the band's work. It is less intense than many of the band's other songs, which use a high-intensity, hardcore style while still remaining very tuneful; "Alien" from *Devotos* is a good example.

ACTIVITY 6.3 *As you listen to CD track 19, "O Meu País" from* Devotos, *note the contrast between the medium tempo rock ballad style and the content of the lyrics, and the growing intensity of the performance.*

Vivo tão feliz	I live so happily
Esse é meu país	This is my country
E todos que o amam	And everyone that loves it
Sabem a sua fama	Knows of its fame
De país do carnaval	As the country of Carnaval
Da selva mundial	Of the global forest
Do rei do futebol	Of the king of football (soccer)
Do "extermínio de menor"	Of "the extermination of minors"
Sabemos do presente	We know about the present
Qual será nosso futuro	What will be our future?
Os menores estão morrendo	The children are dying
Que país inseguro	What an insecure country
Eu já disse isso a você	I've told you this already
Não adianta esquecer	It's no use to forget
Eu vou sempre te lembrar	I'll keep reminding you
Só me deixe expressar	Just let me express myself
Não canto só pra mim	I don't sing just for myself
Canto pra você	I sing for you

Igualdade e consciência	Equality and conscience/ consciousness
É o que nós devemos ter	Is what we should have
O futuro é inseguro	The future is uncertain/ insecure
O caminho obscuro	The road is dark
Mas tem solução	But there is a solution
Vamos todos dar as mãos	Let's all work together

The gentle rock/ballad style may seem at first to be a jarring contrast with the lyrics, which address the serious issue of the assassination of street children in Brazil's major cities, a problem that has attracted international attention. But ultimately the message of the song is a hopeful one.

FACES DO SUBÚRBIO: RAP AND *EMBOLADA* FROM THE ALTO JOSÉ DO PINHO

The hardcore style represented by Devotos is not the only one to be cultivated in the highly active musical community of Alto José do Pinho. The rap group Faces do Subúrbio (Figure 6.6) has attracted national attention for its shows and its three CDs, two self-titled CDs in 1997 (independent) and 1998 (MZA Music) and *Como é triste de olhar* (What a sad sight) (2000, MZA Music), which was nominated for a 2001 Latin Grammy in the best rap/hip-hop album category. The group includes Zé Brown and Tiger, voice and *pandeiro*; DJ KSB, turntables; Oni, guitar and *viola* (10-string steel-string guitar); Marcelo Massacre, bass; and Garnizé, drums. "Faces of the suburb," the literal translation of the group's name, refers to the sort of working-class and low-income suburbs that surround Recife.

Garnizé was featured along with the group's music in the documentary film *O Rap do Pequeno Príncipe Contra as Almas Sebosas* (The Little Prince's Rap Against the Wicked Souls), by Paulo Caldas and Marcelo Luna. The film follows the diverging paths of two youths from a rough Recife suburb, one of which leads to crime and ruin and the other (Garnizé's) to a positive life based on music. See the web site for further information.

FIGURE 6.6 *Tiger (left) and Zé Brown of Faces do Subúrbio.* *(Photo by Arnaldo Carvalho, Agência Lumiar de Fotografia, www.lumiarfoto.com.br.)*

Brazilian rap may sound to outsiders like the imitation of a style created in the United States, but that first impression is deceptive. While some of the style comes from rap, the verbal artistry and the rhythm of the vocals have deep roots in the Northeast region. Vocalists Zé Brown and Tiger move smoothly between rap and the traditional *embolada* style of singing, in which street poets improvise verses to a beat kept on the *pandeiro*, and the rural *toada* style, which has quick vibrato and an upward whoop at the end of phrases reminiscent of the *aboio*, or cattle call. Their lyrics portray everyday life in Recife in catalogs of place names and in narratives of violence and hope intended to increase listeners' awareness of the challenges faced by the underclass. Guitarist Oni plays both electric guitar and *viola*, which is heard along with turntable scratching.

The group attracted press attention in 1997 when their show was stopped by police who objected to their song "Homens Fardados" ("Uniformed Men," included on their 1998 CD), which criticized police violence. They continue to be engaged in community issues in the Alto José do Pinho neighborhood, and they participate in the Acorda Povo project. In 2005 they released another independent CD, *Perito em Rima* (*Expert in Rhyme*).

ACTIVITY 6.4 *As you listen to CD track 20, "Perito em Rima" by Faces do Subúrbio, notice the viola in the opening of the track as electronic sounds fade in to make the transition to the strong beat. Make a list of similarities and differences between this song and rap styles you are familiar with.*

A rima é pra quem sabe rimar	Rhyme is for him who knows how to rhyme
Quem quer ser mais do que Deus	Whoever wants to be greater than God
Fica pior do que está	Ends up worse than he was before
Iniciei forjando a mente para a rima	I started forming my mind for rhyming
Sem participar de nenhuma oficina	Without taking any classes
Com auto-estima sempre acima	With self-esteem always high
Tá disciplinado aqui em cima	It's disciplined up here
Rap embolada repente, minha obra-prima	*Rap embolada repente,* my masterpiece
Perito em rima é improviso poesia sina	Expert in rhyme it's improvisation poetry fate
Representando com muito orgulho	Representing with much pride
A nação nordestina	The Northeastern nation

See the web site for the complete lyrics, which include many regional references. At around 2:00, listen for the *pandeiro* accompaniment style for *embolada* as the opening refrain returns. At around 3:30, listen for the vocal phrases that start with a sustained high tone—this is typical of *embolada*. For another example of the *embolada* style, see the CD that accompanies vol. 2 of *The Garland Encyclopedia of World Music*.

FIGURE 6.7 *DJ Dolores e Orchestra Santa Massa perform in Old Recife. (L to R) Isaar França, Maciel Salustiano, DJ Dolores, Mr. Jam (Jamilson Monteiro).* (Photo by Chico Barros, Agência Lumiar de Fotografia, www.lumiarfoto.com.br.)

DJ DOLORES E ORCHESTRA SANTA MASSA: ELECTRONIC *MARACATU*

DJ Dolores is the artistic name of Hélder Aragão, who, with his band Orchestra Santa Massa (Figure 6.7), creates music that incorporates sampled and electronic sounds with the sounds and performance practice of traditional Northeastern music. The name "Dolores" is the plural of the Spanish *dolor*, which means pain or sorrow. He was involved both musically and as a graphic artist with the beginning of the *mangue* movement, and has created music for films (such as *Enjaulado* and *O Rap do Pequeno Príncipe Contra as Almas Sebosas*, both of which include other collaborators) and plays (*A Máquina*). Today, he is one of the best-known figures of the Recife scene, nationally and internationally.

DJ Dolores thinks of electronic music as a medium, not an aesthetic. In other words, the fact that he uses electronic tools—loops, filters, delays, samples—to manipulate sound doesn't predetermine the style of the music he makes. In his early projects he used mostly environmental sounds; his technology was a two-channel office recording machine. He did the remix of Otto's "O Celular de Naná" (on *Changez Tout*, Trama 2000) using very simple software, starting from separate tracks provided by the record company. He currently uses a laptop to manipulate samples (Lusk 2003), but when we talked in 2001, he was using the AKAI MIDI Production Center 2000.

The "instrument" allows a large number of samples to be looped and combined, but DJ Dolores opts for simplicity with short loops of one or two measures.

> A short loop is more hypnotic. The simpler the better, the more perfect. This simplicity is difficult to achieve, because when a drummer arrives to record a sample and it turns out supersophisticated, it's tiring and doesn't work when you repeat it.

The CD *Contraditório?* (Contradictory?) by DJ Dolores and Orchestra Santa Massa attracted much international attention after its Brazilian release on the Candeeiro label was distributed by Stern's Music, which has long been involved with global/popular music (sound clips from all of the tracks are available at the Stern's site; see the web site for links).

ACTIVITY 6.5 *As you listen to CD track 21, "Samba de Dez Linhas" by DJ Dolores e Orchestra Santa Massa from* Contraditório?, *note the alternation between poetry and percussion, as in traditional* maracatu rural. *This song adapts the traditional* maracatu rural *to an electronic context: the percussion parts blend electronic beats and live percussion with* rabeca *played by Maciel Salustiano, son of Mestre Manoel Salustiano, who sings verses in* maracatu *style when the percussion pauses. Just as in traditional* maracatu rural, *the instrumental refrain is played on trombone; here, unlike the traditional practice,* rabeca *doubles the refrain. The title refers to the poetic form of the lyrics (ten-line* samba*).*

É um vaqueiro encourado	A	It's one leather-clad cowboy
Dois touro brabo correndo	B	Two wild bulls running
Três contravento moendo	B	Three wind-powered mills grinding
Quatro cego malcriado	A	Four rude blind men
Cinco dúzia de aleijado	A	Five dozen cripples
Seis velha pedindo esmola	C	Six old ladies begging
[fifth and sixth lines repeated]		
Sete pásso na gaiola	C	Seven birds in the cage
Oito carga de aguardente	D	Eight shots of cane rum
Nove velha sem ter dente	D	Nine toothless old ladies
Dez cordas numa viola	C	Ten strings on a viola
Com dez eu pego na casa	A	With ten I start the house
Com vinte assento os esteio	B	With twenty I set the supports
Com trinta eu parto o meio	B	With twenty I divide it in the middle
Quarenta eu não me atraso	A	Forty I don't delay
Com cinquenta eu cavo a base	A	With fifty I dig the foundation
Sessenta a porta e a janela	C	Sixty the door and the window
Setenta eu obro a tigela	C	With seventy I raise the walls
Oitenta eu ripo e amarro	D	Eighty I raise the roof beams and tie the tiles
Com noventa eu bato o barro	D	With ninety I line it with clay
E com cem estou dentro dela	C	And with a hundred I'm inside it
Lá na Torre Malakoff	A	There in Malakoff Tower
Vi acender uma luz	B	I saw a light go on
Na Rua do Bom Jesus	B	On the Rua do Bom Jesus
Afinei minha rabeca		I tuned my rabeca
Fui para a Rua da Moeda		I went to the Rua da Moeda
Tocar com muita harmonia	C	To play with much harmony

[fifth and sixth lines repeated]		
Lá tem gente todo dia	C	It's crowded there every day
Vai até de madrugada	D	Until dawn
Tomando muita cachaça	D′	Drinking lots of cachaça
No Bar da Cachaçaria	C	At the Cachaçaria Bar

The rhyme scheme is the same as that used by Siba and Barachinha in "Catimbó" (see Chapter 4). The lyrics of the first two stanzas form a numbered progression. The first stanza counts from one to ten in images on a rural theme. The second describes the construction of a house while counting from 10 to 100. The third stanza refers to Old Recife, where many performances take place, and departs from the rhyme scheme slightly. Note the references in the third stanza to Old Recife and *a Rua do Bom Jesus*, a section of Recife and the name of the street where the first New World synagogue was located, which were mentioned at the beginning of Chapter 1. Further information about this part of Recife is available on the companion web site. This intertwining of past and present is emblematic of the way tradition and modernity are in constant dialogue, not only in the musical community and cityscape of Recife, but in Brazil as a whole.

DJ Dolores views his work as more than a simple combination of traditional music with electronic music.

> It's very easy to take a sample of a *forró* beat and combine it with a sophisticated synthesizer, or take a jungle beat and combine it with *rabeca*—this is very easy. It's a question of approach, of how you position yourself within it. If the result is simply the mixture of a roots thing with a techno thing, I think that's dumb. If you have some previous education about the style, you can think about the structure of the music.

There are many discussions within the band about the structure of pieces. Some members are used to a form consisting of a theme that is sung and then played instrumentally. DJ Dolores often wants to extend the repetition for a longer time.

> Sometimes the music needs to have something that repeats for a long time because that's part of the conception of the music. To create a dialogue between the structures, in the way you compose this hybrid song, is more important than simply mixing the *rabeca* with an electronic beat.

DJ Dolores is attracted to traditional musics that have a strong beat and lots of repetition, styles that combine well with his electronic tools. When I asked what kinds of traditional music interest him most, he replied:

> *Maracatu rural* is very interesting, I think. Besides being very repetitive, it works with the idea of different tempos. The percussion is very fast, double the tempo of the click of the voice or the instruments. I think this is very interesting. Anything with powerful drums is interesting.

DJ Dolores addressed in a nuanced way the question of the rise in self-esteem on the part of Northeasterners as a result of the increased media attention brought to the region by the *mangue* movement.

> I think this idea of self-esteem is something that has developed over the last ten years and is related to the artistic and commercial success of so-called *mangue-beat*. This has inspired the entire Northeast. In Maceió, Fortaleza, Sergipe, and Bahia, you'll find excellent things such as Cidadão Instigado [a project led by Fernando Catatau, who collaborated with DJ Dolores on the music for *A Máquina*, in Fortaleza] and Cravo e Carbono [a band from Belém led by guitarist Pio Lobato, who plays the local *guitarrada* style], which discovered their own path inspired by the essence of Chico [Science], making use of tradition, doing something new of your own inspired by tradition, to things with a nationalistic, almost extreme-right aspect.
>
> Author: For example?
>
> For example, there is a very common sentiment here in Recife: "I'm proud to be a Northeasterner." I think this kind of thing is somewhat dangerous. It's the bad side of the coin, in the sense that every mass culture has a good side and it has this distorted and dumb side on which one thinks that his or her state is better than another, that his or her city is better than another. This localist sentiment is exactly the opposite of the *mangue* story. There was always a vocation to be cosmopolitan. There was never a dumb discourse of conflict because of a city or a postal code.

The other members of Orchestra Santa Massa have continued to lead and participate in other musical projects. Maciel Salustiano was part of the band Chão e Chinelo, which recorded the independent CD *Loa do Boi Meia Noite* in 1998, and currently leads the group Maciel Salu e O Terno do Terreiro, which recorded the CD *A Pisada é Assim* in 2003. Guitarist Fábio Trummer led the band Eddie, whose song "Quando a maré encher" has been covered by Nação Zumbi (*Rádio S.AMB.A*) and the late Cássia Eller (*Acústico MTV*, 2001). Drummer Mr. Jam (Jamilson Monteiro) is one of the busiest rhythm section players in the Recife scene, whose other projects include the CD *Aboiando a Vaca Mecânica* by Lula Queiroga. Current information about DJ Dolores's projects is available on the web site.

COMADRE FLORZINHA AND WOMEN'S PARTICIPATION IN THE RECIFE SCENE

Vocalist Isaar França and percussionist Karina Buhr, who have collaborated extensively with DJ Dolores, were part of the all-female group Comadre Florzinha, which released a self-titled CD of reinterpretations of traditional music in 1999 (Fig. 6.8). In a conversation we had about the Recife scene, Karina Buhr touched on one of the main themes that has appeared already in this section: that bands from Recife, no matter how creative, are continually categorized as regional rather than national. Bands from Rio de Janeiro or São Paulo are more easily perceived as "national."

Buhr's story exemplifies the upsurge in interest in traditional music on the part of young people in Recife during the 1990s. As the decade began, she was dancing with the Balé Popular do Recife. Then she met Siba, saw *cavalo-marinho* performed in the rural areas outside Recife, and joined a *cavalo-marinho* group that was formed by members of the band Mestre Ambrósio and their friends. It was unusual for women to participate in rural groups, but she learned some of the characters and the percussion parts, including the *mineiro* (cylindrical rattle). She played the *baiana* role in Mestre Salustiano's Maracatu Piaba de Ouro, a *maracatu rural* group, but was not allowed to play percussion in public performances. Salustiano even commented that *maracatu rural* was better in the days when men played the *baiana* role. After playing *alfaia* (bass drum) in the Maracatu Estrela Brilhante, a new group in the *maracatu de nação* style, and in the rock band Eddie, she met Renata Mattar, who played *sanfona*, and decided to form an all-female band, Comadre Florzinha, in order to showcase her composing, arranging, and percussion playing.

Buhr felt it was important to start the group to counter the way women's participation in traditional genres was discouraged except for certain singing and dancing roles. Incidents like the following strengthened her determination:

FIGURE 6.8 *Karina Buhr plays* alfaia *and sings during a performance in Olinda in 2004.* (*Photo by Jason Gardner.*)

The first time I went to play the *mineiro* [in a *cavalo-marinho* performance in the country], the guy who was playing the *mineiro* took a break. Siba was playing *rabeca*, and he called me to play the *mineiro* because he knew I knew how to play, but the other people there didn't know it. I started to play, and everything stopped. Everything stopped, and a Galante came over and took the *mineiro* from my hand and started playing—incorrectly. He took it out of my hand without asking and started playing incorrectly until the other player came back. That's what it was like.

In the Recife rock scene, women participated mostly as singers and dancers, and in the Maracatu Estrela Brilhante, she had to persist in her demands to play percussion in public performances along with two other female percussionists. The band Comadre Florzinha provided Buhr, Mattar, Isaar França, Telma César, and Maria Helena the chance to perform without gender-based restrictions, and to tour Europe, Canada, and the United States.

CONCLUSION

The musicians discussed in this chapter manage to be both committed to the city of Recife and its culture and extremely aware of the most advanced trends in global popular music. In Recife's music scene, living oral traditions coexist and interact with cutting-edge popular music experiments. In the founding image of the *mangue* movement, a satellite antenna stuck in the mud of fertile tidal marshes energizes the city's cultural circuits (and in local slang, to be *antenado*, literally "antenna'd," means to be plugged into the global flow of information). This has attracted many music fans and scholars from elsewhere in Brazil and abroad; see, for example, Galinsky (2002), the first in-depth study of *mangue* in English. The vitality and diversity of the Recife music scene demonstrate that the global spread of technology and mass media is not simply a one-way process in which local musics inevitably get marginalized. Visionary musicians, artists, and producers, like those of the Recife scene, can adapt the flow of outside information to their own ends.

In a sense, the recent history of the Recife popular music scene mirrors larger trends in Brazilian music that may be more apparent to readers now than they were when they were previewed in the preface. Brazilian musicians have always cultivated a sense of national identity, modified it with the accents of regional traditions, and blended it with musics from outside Brazil. Think of Pixinguinha blending *choro* with the hot music he heard in Paris in the 1920s; Carmen Miranda bringing *samba* to Hollywood; Luiz Gonzaga making the *baião* into a national style; Tom Jobim and João Gilberto adapting jazz harmonies to fit their intimate version of *samba*; Roberto Carlos touching millions of Brazilian hearts with sentimental *boleros*. Each time a Brazilian musician decides to express himself or herself in song—and each time a listener makes Brazilian music a part of his or her life—a new chapter is added to this story.

Glossary

agogô double metal bell

alfaia large bass drum

baião Northeastern Brazilian musical genre popularized by Luiz Gonzaga

baiano up-tempo duple meter, northeastern Brazilian genre

bateria the percussion ensemble that accompanies the samba school

berimbau musical bow used to accompany *capoeira*

boi ox

bossa nova intimate form of *samba* developed in late 1950s in Rio de Janeiro

brega unrefined, corny; sentimental pop music genre

bumba-meu-boi dramatic dance centering around the death and rebirth of an ox

caboclo de lança warrior figure in *maracatu de baque solto*

caipira relating to rural South-Central Brazil

caixa snare drum

candomblé Afro-Brazilian religion that involves spirit possession

capoeira dance/martial art/game with musical accompaniment

carioca from Rio de Janeiro

Carnaval carnival, celebrated on the three days preceding the start of Lent and during the preceding weeks

cavalo-marinho form of *bumba-meu-boi* performed in Pernambuco

cavaquinho small guitar used in samba

choro primarily instrumental genre with long, syncopated melodies, often performed with light samba feel

cuíca friction drum

escola de samba samba school

forró Northeast Brazilian dance music featuring accordion, *zabumba*, triangle

ganzá cylindrical rattle

guitarra electric guitar

MPB *Música Popular Brasileira*; in 1960s, popular music of high artistic achievement that drew from Brazilian musical traditions and used acoustic instruments; later, includes rock and other international elements

malandro urban hustler

mangue literally a mangrove marsh; the name of the Recife popular music movement which began in the early 1990s

maracatu Afro-Brazilian genre practiced in Recife and surrounding areas in two forms: *maracatu de baque virado* and *maracatu de baque solto*; the differences are explained in the text

mestre master performer

moda-de-viola long narrative songs in *caipira* music

morro hillside neighborhood, or *favela*, of Rio de Janeiro

mulata Brazilian woman of mixed descent

música caipira rural music of South-Central Brazil

música sertaneja Brazilian "country" music sung by vocal duos

música gaúcha music of Southern Brazil, especially of Rio Grande do Sul

orixá deity in Afro-Brazilian religion

pagode backyard samba style

pandeiro tambourine

quilombo escaped slave community

rabeca fiddle

reco-reco scraper made of bamboo or metal

repinique drum used in samba *bateria*

samba national dance/music genre of Afro-Brazilian origin

samba-canção samba-song

samba-de-roda circle samba of Bahia

samba-enredo Carnaval theme samba
samba-exaltação samba in praise of Brazil
sambista performer of samba
sanfona accordion
sertão semi-arid backlands of Northeast Brazil
surdo large bass drum
tamborim small tambourine
toada rural song genre, often religious
Tropicália experimental popular music movement in 1967–9
viola guitar with five double-coursed steel strings
violão six-string guitar with nylon strings
zabumba bass drum used in *forró*

References

Albuquerque, Durval Muniz de, Jr. 1999. *A Invenção do Nordeste e Outras Artes.* Recife: Editora Massangana/São Paulo: Cortez.

Anderson, David E. 1990. "Melbourne, Montreal, Seattle Among 'Most Livable' Cities." [Wire service report on the study by Population Crisis Committee, now Population Action International.] UPI, November 20. http://www.library.ohiou.edu/indopubs/1990/11/21/0002.html

Araújo, Samuel M. 1988. "Brega: Music and Conflict in Urban Brazil." *Latin American Music Review* 9/1: 50–89.

BBC. 2005. "Q&A: World Social Forum 2005." http://news.bbc.co.uk/1/hi/business/4204829.stm

Béhague, Gerard. 1973. "Bossa and Bossas: Recent Changes in Brazilian Urban Popular Music." *Ethnomusicology* 17/2: 209–33.

———. 2001. "Brazil: Art Music." In *The New Grove Dictionary of Music and Musicians,* vol. 4, 2nd ed. (London: Macmillan), 268–271.

Browning, Barbara. 1995. *Samba: Resistance in Motion.* Bloomington: Indiana University Press.

Bueno, André Paula. 2001. *Bumba-boi Maranhense em São Paulo.* São Paulo: Nankin.

Câmara Cascudo, Luís da. 1972. *Dicionário do Folclore Brasileiro.* 3rd ed. Rio de Janeiro: Tecnoprint.

Carvalho, Martha Ulhôa de. 1990. "*Canção da América*—style and emotion in Brazilian popular song." *Popular Music* 9/3: 321–49.

Castro, Ruy. 2000. *Bossa Nova: The Story of the Brazilian Music That Seduced the World.* Translation of *Chega de Saudade: A História e as Histórias da Bossa Nova* (São Paulo: Companhia das Letras, 1990) by Lysa Salsbury. Chicago: A Cappella.

Cazes, Henrique. 1998. *Choro: Do Quintal ao Municipal.* São Paulo: Editora 34.

Connell, Andrew Mark. 2002. "Jazz Brasileiro? *Música instrumental brasileira* and the representation of identity in Rio de Janeiro." Ph.D. Dissertation, University of California at Los Angeles.

Corrêa, Roberto. 2000. *A Arte de Pontear Viola.* Brasília, Curitiba: Ed. Autor.

Crook, Larry. 1993. "Black Consciousness, Samba-Reggae, and the Re-Africanization of Bahian Carnival Music in Brazil." *the world of music* 35/2: 90–108.

Dent, Alexander S. 2003. "Country Critics: *Música Caipira* and the Production of Locality in Brazil." Ph.D. dissertation, University of Chicago.

Donato, Dagoberto. n.d. Text about Mundo Livre S/A's "O Outro Mundo de Xicão Xukuru" that appeared on the Trama web site and was included in a press release about the song.

Downey, Greg. 2002. "Listening to Capoeira: Phenomenology, Embodiment, and the Materiality of Music." *Ethnomusicology* 46/3: 487–509.

———. 2005. *Learning Capoeira: Lessons in Cunning from an Afro-Brazilian Art.* New York: Oxford University Press.

Dunn, Christopher. 2001. *Brutality Garden: Tropicália and the Emergence of a Brazilian Counterculture.* Chapel Hill, NC: University of North Carolina Press.

Ferreira dos Santos, Joaquim. n.d. "Roberto Carlos." Entry in the *Dicionário Cravo Albin da Música Popular Brasileira,* www.dicionariompb.com.br.

Fred04. 2004. "Dez anos não são dez dias." www.manguetronic.com.br, in the section entitled "Verbum."

Galinsky, Philip. 1996. "Co-option, Cultural Resistance, and Afro-Brazilian Identity: A History of the *Pagode* Samba Movement in Rio de Janeiro." *Latin American Music Review* 17/2: 120–49.

———. 2002. *"Maracatu Atômico": Tradition, Modernity, and Postmodernity in the Mangue Movement of Recife, Brazil.* New York: Routledge.

Gilliam, Angela, and Onik'a Gilliam. 1999. "Odyssey: Negotiating the Subjectivity of *Mulata* Identity in Brazil." *Latin American Perspectives* 26/3: 60–84.

Gilman, Bruce. 1996. "Forward to the Past" [Discusses Roberto Carlos in the context of the 5-CD reissue *30 Anos da Jovem Guarda*]. *BRAZZIL* online magazine, www.brazil-brasil.com/cvrjan96.htm.

———. 1998. "EG = mc^2." Interview with Egberto Gismonti. *BRAZZIL* online magazine www.brazil-brasil.com/musjun98.htm.

Goyena, Héctor Luis. 2000. "Milonga." In *Diccionario de la Música Española e Hispanoamericana* (Spain: Sociedad General de Autores y Editores), vol. 7, pp. 582–3.

Guerra-Peixe, César. 1980. *Maracatus do Recife.* 2nd ed. São Paulo: Irmãos Vitale.

Guerreiro, Goli. 2000. *A Trama dos Tambores: a Música Afro-pop de Salvador.* São Paulo: Editora 34.

Hagedorn, Katherine. 2001. *Divine Utterances: The Performance of Afro-Cuban Santería.* Washington, D.C.: Smithsonian Institution Press.

Joaquim, Luiz. 2000. "Ministério da Cultura quer transformar o maracatu na imagem do Brasil no exterior" (Ministry of Culture wants to transform the *maracatu* into the image of Brasil overseas). *Jornal do Commercio* (Recife), December 22.

Lewis, J. Lowell. 1992. *Ring of Liberation: Deceptive Discourse in Brazilian Capoeira.* Chicago: University of Chicago Press.

Livingston, Tamara. 1999. "Music Revivals: Towards a General Theory." *Ethnomusicology* 43/1: 66–85.

Louzeiro, José. 1987. *Devotos do Ódio.* São Paulo: Global Editora.

Lucas, Maria Elizabeth. 2000. "Gaucho Musical Regionalism." *British Journal of Ethnomusicology* 9/1: 41–60.

———. 2002. Review of *Brazilian Popular Music & Globalization,* ed. Perrone and Dunn. *Notes* 59/2: 323–4.

Lusk, Jon. 2003. "BBC—Radio 3—Awards for World Music 2004—DJ Dolores and Orchestra Santa Massa." www.bbc.co.uk/radio3/world/awards2004/profile_djdolores.shtml

McCann, Bryan. 2004. *Hello, Hello Brazil: Popular Music in the Making of Modern Brazil.* Durham: Duke University Press.

McGowan, Chris, and Ricardo Pessanha. 1998. *The Brazilian Sound: Samba, Bossa Nova, and the Popular Music of Brazil.* Philadelphia: Temple University Press.

Moore, Robin. 1997. *Nationalizing Blackness: Afrocubanismo and Artistic Revolution in Havana, 1920–1940.* Pittsburgh: University of Pittsburgh Press.

Moraes, Mestre. 1996. Liner notes accompanying the CD *Capoeira Angola from Salvador, Brazil by the Grupo de Capoeira Angola Pelourinho.* Smithsonian/Folkways SF CD 40465.

Moura, Milton Araújo. 2001. "World of Fantasy, Fantasy of the World: Geographic Space and the Representation of Identity in the Carnival of Salvador, Bahia." In Charles Perrone and Christopher Dunn, eds., *Brazilian Popular Music & Globalization* (Gainesville, FL: University Press of Florida), 161–76.

Murphy, John Patrick. 1994. "Performing a Moral Vision: An Ethnography of Cavalo-Marinho, A Brazilian Musical Drama." Ph.D. dissertation, Columbia University.

———. 1997. "The *Rabeca* and Its Music, Old and New, in Pernambuco, Brazil." *Latin American Music Review* 18/2: 147–72.

Oliveira Pinto, Tiago de. 1996. "Musical Difference, Competition, and Conflict: The Maracatu Groups in the Pernambuco Carnival, Brazil." *Latin American Music Review* 17/2: 97–119.

Oliven, Ruben George. 1988. "The Woman Makes (and Breaks) the Man": The Masculine Imagery in Brazilian Popular Music." *Latin American Music Review* 9/1: 90–108.

Perrone, Charles A. 1989. *Masters of Contemporary Brazilian Song: MPB 1965–1985*. Austin: University of Texas Press.

———. 2001. "Myth, Melopeia, and Mimesis: *Black Orpheus*, *Orfeu*, and Internationalization in Brazilian Popular Music." In Perrone and Christopher Dunn, eds., *Brazilian Popular Music and Globalization* (Gainesville, FL: University Press of Florida), 46–71.

Rabben, Linda. 2004. *Brazil's Indians and the Onslaught of Civilization: The Yanomami and the Kayapó*. Seattle: University of Washington Press.

Raphael, Allison. 1990. "From Popular Culture to Microenterprise: The History of Brazilian Samba Schools." *Latin American Music Review* 11/1: 73–83.

Ratliff, Ben. 2001. "Recife Resounds With the Futurist Mix of a Rock Hero." *The New York Times*, April 24.

Real, Katarina. 1990. *O Folclore no Carnaval do Recife*. Recife: Editora Massangana.

Reily, Suzel Ana. 1992. "*Música Sertaneja* and Migrant Identity: The Stylistic Development of a Brazilian Genre." *Popular Music* 11/3: 337–58.

———. 1996. "Tom Jobim and the Bossa Nova Era." *Popular Music* 15/1: 1–16.

———. 1998. "Brazil: Central and Southern Areas." In *The Garland Encyclopedia of World Music*, Vol. 2: *South America, Mexico, Central America, and the Caribbean*. Eds. Dale A. Olsen and Daniel E. Sheehy. New York: Garland, 300–322.

———. 2002. *Voices of the Magi: Enchanted Journeys in Southeast Brazil*. Chicago: University of Chicago Press

Rohter, Larry. 2003. "Songs by a Man with Heart Mean Christmas in Brazil." *The New York Times*, December 24.

Sanches, Pedro Alexandre. 2000. *Tropicalismo: Decadência Bonita do Samba*. São Paulo: Boitempo Editorial.

Sandroni, Carlos. 2001. *Feitiço Decente: Transformações do Samba no Rio de Janeiro (1917–1933)*. Rio de Janeiro: Jorge Zahar Editora/Editora UFRJ.

Scheper-Hughes, Nancy. 1992. *Death Without Weeping: The Violence of Everyday Life in Brazil*. Berkeley: University of California Press.

Seeger, Anthony. 1998. "The Tropical-Forest Region." In *The Garland Encyclopedia of World Music, Volume 2: South America, Mexico, Central America, and the Caribbean*. Eds. Dale A. Olsen and Daniel E. Sheehy. New York: Garland, 123–36.

Severiano, Jairo, and Zuza Homem de Mello. 2002. *A Canção no Tempo: 85 Anos de Músicas Brasileiras*. 2 volumes. 5th edition. São Paulo: Editora 34.

Shaw, Lisa. 1999. *The Social History of the Brazilian Samba*. Aldershot, England, and Brookfield, VT: Ashgate.

Siba. 2002. Liner notes to *fuloresta do samba*. Terreiro Discos TDCD 050.

Souza, Tárik de, and Ary Vasconcelos, Roberto M. Moura, João Máximo, Roberto Muggiati, Luiz Carlos Mansur, Turíbio Santos, Affonso R. Sant'Anna, and Rita Cáurio. 1988. *Brasil Musical/Musical Brazil*. Rio de Janeiro: Art Bureau Representações e Edições de Arte.

Teles, José. 2000. *Do Frevo ao Manguebeat*. São Paulo: Editora 34.

Tesser, Neil. 1989. Liner notes to *The Girl from Ipanema: The Bossa Nova Years*. Verve 823 611–2.

Time magazine. 2001. "Music Goes Global." *Time*, September, time.com/time/musicgoesglobal/la/mmax.html.

Tinhorão, José Ramos. 1986. *Pequena História da Música Popular: Da Modinha ao Tropicalismo*. 5th edition. São Paulo: Art Editora.

———. 1998. *História Social da Música Popular Brasileira*. São Paulo: Editora 34.

Turner, Terence. 1995. "Social Body and Embodied Subject: Bodiliness, Subjectivity, and Sociality among the Kayapó." *Cultural Anthropology* 10/2: 143–70.

———. 1999. "Indigenous Rights, Environmental Protection, and the Struggle over Forest Resources in the Amazon: The Case of the Brazilian Kayapo." In *Earth, Air, Fire, Water: Humanistic Studies of the Environment*, ed. Jill Ker Conway, Kenneth Keniston, and Leo Marx (Amherst: University of Massachusetts Press), 145–69.

Veloso, Caetano. 2001. "Carmen Mirandadada." Translated by Robert Myers and Charles A. Perrone. In Perrone and Christopher Dunn, eds., *Brazilian Popular Music & Globalization* (Gainesville, FL: University Press of Florida), 39–45.

Verswijver, Gustaaf, ed. 1992. *Kaiapó Amazonia: The Art of Body Decoration*. Gent: Snoeck-Ducaju & Zoon.

Vianna, Hermano. 1999. *The Mystery of Samba: Popular Music & National Identity in Brazil*. Edited and translated by John Charles Chasteen. Chapel Hill: University of North Carolina Press.

Resources

Listening

Afro Brasil (Verve Polygram, 1992).

Beleza Tropical 2: Novo! Mais! Melhor!, compiled by David Byrne (Luaka Bop, 1998).

Bossa Nova Brasil (Verve Polygram, 1992).

Brasil: a century of song. 4-CD set. (Blue Jackel, 1995). Out of print, but may be available used or in libraries.

Brazil Classics 1: Beleza Tropical, compiled by David Byrne (Fly/Sire, 1989).

Brazil Classics 2: O Samba, compiled by David Byrne (Luaka Bop/Sire, 1989).

Brazil Classics 3: Forró etc., compiled by David Byrne (Luaka Bop/Sire, 1991).

Brazil: Forró, Music for Maids and Taxi Drivers (Rounder CD 5044, 1989).

Brazil: Roots-Samba (Rounder CD 5045, 1989).

Caipiríssimo: Clássicos e Jóias da Música Caipira (Kurarup Discos KCD 171, 2002).

Capoeira Angola 2: Brincando na Roda, Grupo de Capoeira Angola Pelourinho (Smithsonian Folkways Recordings SFW CD 40488, 2003).

Capoeira, Samba, Candomblé (Museum Collection Berlin CD 16, 1990).

Carnival in Pernambuco/Brasil (Museum Edition Hamburg, 1992). Includes *maracatu de baque solto* and *maracatu de baque virado*.

Desde que o Choro é Choro: A Brief History of Choro. Henrique Cazes & Família Violão (Kuarup Discos KCD 071).

The Discoteca Collection: Missão de Pesquisas Folclóricas (Rykodisc RCD 10403, 1997).

The Garland Encyclopedia of World Music, Vol. 2: South America, Mexico, Central America, and the Caribbean. Eds: Dale A. Olsen and Daniel E. Sheehy. New York: Garland, 1998. Accompanying CD.

L.H. Corrêa de Azevedo: Music of Ceará and Minas Gerais (Rykodisc RCD 10404, 1997).

Nordeste Brasil (Verve Polygram, 1992).

The Rough Guide to the Music of Brazil (World Music Network RGNET 1021 CD).
The Rough Guide to Samba (World Music Network RGNET 1058 CD).
The Rough Guide to the Music of Brazil: Bahia (World Music Network RGNET 1135 CD).
The Rough Guide to Brazilian Hip-Hop (World Music Network RGNET 1141 CD).
The Rough Guide to Brazilian Electronica (World Music Network RGNET 1123 CD).
Samba Brasil (Verve Polygram, 1992). Includes "Aquarela do Brasil" sung by Gal Costa.
Sambas de Enredo 2004 (BMG, 2003).
Saudade em Samba: Brasil 1929–1942 (Kardum/Iris, 1998). Includes the original recording of "Aquarela do Brasil."
This is Samba! Volume 1 (Rounder CD 5091, 2000).
Tropicália Essentials (Hip-O Records 314 546 392 2, 1999).
Unwired: Latin America (World Music Network RGNET 1076 CD).

Viewing

Bossa Nova: Music and Reminiscences (Multicultural Media MCM1005, 1993).
Calle 54 (Burbank, Calif.: Miramax Home Entertainment, Buena Vista Home Entertainment, 2001). This documentary on Latin jazz devotes a chapter to Brazilian pianist Eliane Elias.
Carmen Miranda: Bananas is My Business. Dir. Helena Solberg, 1995. DVD (Fox Lorber, 2002).
The JVC/Smithsonian Folkways Video Anthology of Music and Dance of the Americas: Central and South America. Vol. 5. Washington, D.C.: Smithsonian/Folkways Recordings; Montpelier, VT: Dist. by Multicultural Media, 1995.
The JVC Video Anthology of World Music and Dance: The Americas II. Tokyo: JVC, Victor Company of Japan, 1988; Cambridge, MA: Rounder Records, 1990. Includes sections on *samba, capoeira,* and *candomblé.*
O Velho Amigo: O Universo Musical de Baden Powell. (Universal [France], 2003).
Orfeu Negro. Dir. Marcel Camus, 1959. DVD (The Criterion Collection 48, 1999).
The Spirit of Samba: Black Music of Brazil. Dir. Jeremy Marre, 1982. DVD (Shanachie 1207, 2000).

Other

Allmusic, information on artists, genres, CDs; includes audio samples; free registration: www.allmusic.com

Author's website, with supplementary information and links to artist and record label web sites and audio samples linked to the site for this series, ⟨www.oup.com/us/globalmusic⟩

The Brazilian Sound, information and CD/video/book sales: www.thebraziliansound.com

BrazilMax, guide to travel and culture: www.brazilmax.com

Brazzil magazine, includes articles on music: www.brazzil.com

Cliquemusic, Brazilian commercial CD site in English: www.cliquemusic.com.br/en/home/home.asp

Dicionário Cravo Albin da Música Popular Brasileira, Brazilian popular music dictionary, in Portuguese: www.dicionariompb.com.br

International Capoeira Angola Foundation: www.capoeira.org

Latin American Network Information Center, University of Texas at Austin, Brazil resources: www1.lanic.utexas.edu/la/brazil/

Library of Congress country study for Brazil: lcweb2.loc.gov/frd/cs/brtoc.html

Maria-Brazil, Brazilian culture site with many music-related pages and links: www.maria-brazil.org

Luaka Bop, sample tracks from its Brazilian CDs: www.luakabop.com

Rounder Records, audio samples from its Brazilian CDs: www.rounder.com

Trama Records, artist information in Portuguese and audio samples: www.trama.com.br

Universo Online, Brazil's largest Web portal, offers a content-only subscription (currently $7 per month), which allows access to a searchable archive of thousands of complete tracks in streaming format from all periods of recorded Brazilian music history, including the original recording of "Pelo Telefone" (1917) and many of the songs mentioned in this book; in Portuguese; instructions for subscribing available at author's website: www.uol.com.br

World Music Network, catalog of the Rough Guide series, with audio samples: www.worldmusic.net/catalogue/latin.html

Index

Accordion, xvi. *See also sanfona de oito baixos, gaita*
Acselrad, Maria, 86
Afoxé, 21
Albuquerque, Durval Muniz de, 100
Alcione, 23
Almeida, Mauro de, 9
Alves, Ataulfo, 12
Amado, Jorge, 44
Amaral, Alício, 74
Amélia, Tia, 35
Andrade, Mário de, 14, 15, 36
Andrade, Oswald de, 14, 15, 46
Antunes, Arnaldo, 132
"Aquarela do Brasil," 16, 17, 147
Aragão, Jorge, 23, 25
Araújo, Severino, 34
Arlindo dos Oito Baixos, xvi, 35, 100–108
Art music, 35–36
"Asa Branca," 98, 127
Axé music, 22, 25, 129
Azevedo, Waldir, 33

Babenco, Hector, 146
Bachianas Brasileiras, 36
Baião, xiii, 80, 94, 95, 143
Baiana, João da, 8
Bambaataa, Afrika, 133
Bandolim, Jacob do, 32, 33
Barachinha, 91–94, 154
Barbosa, Adoniran, 23
Barroso, Ari, 16, 17, 23, 47, 147
Barroso, Inezita, 114, 117
Bastos, Ronaldo, 49
Bateria, 1, 10
Batista, Mestre, xvi, 72–74
Beatles, The, 46, 47, 129
Béhague, Gerard, xvi, 37
Belém, Fafá de, 70
Ben Jor, Jorge, 26, 133, 139
Berimbau, 59–61
Bethânia, Maria, 23, 53
Bide, 9
Bloco afro, 21
Boi-Bumbá, 70
Bolla 8, Gilmar, 134
Borges, Lô, 49
Borges, Márcio, 49
Borghetti, Renato, 122, 125–28
Bosco, João, 48
Bôscoli, Ronaldo, 38, 45–6
Bossa nova, xiii, xiv, 6, 24, 36–46, 50; *bossa nova clave*, 43; and cosmopolitanism, 131; and modernizing Brazil, 44–6
Brandão, Leci, 8, 23
Brant, Fernando, 49
Brega, xiii, 23, 50–54
Brown, Carlinhos, 22, 47, 132
Brown, Celo, 144
Brown, James, 133
Brown, Zé, 148, 149
Browning, Barbara, 63
Buarque, Chico, 23, 26, 47–50
Buarque de Holanda, Sérgio, 14
Bueno, André, 86
Buhr, Karina, 156–58
Bumba-meu-boi, xiii, 70–72
Byrne, David, 49

Caboclinhos, 4, 146
Caipira, Música, xiv, 109–17, 130; duo style, 113–14
Caju e Castanha, 138
Caldas, Luiz, 22
Caldas, Paulo, 148
Calixto, Zé, 35, 126–27
Callado, Joaquim Antônio, 31
Camargo, Zezé di, e Luciano, 119
Candomblé, 8, 21
Canhoto, Leo, e Robertinho, 118

Cannibal, 144
Cannibalist Manifesto, 14, 46
Cantoria, 113
Capoeira Angola, xiii, xiv, 47, 55–63, 134; *Capoeira Atual*, 62; *Capoeira Regional*, 62
Cardoso de Meneses, Carolina, 35
Carimbó, 70
Cariocas, Os, 43
Carlos, Erasmo, 26, 51
Carlos, Roberto, xiii, 26, 47, 48, 51–54, 158
Carnaval, 4, 19, 28; in Recife, 1, 2, 4; in Rio de Janeiro, 4–6, 9, 19; in Salvador, 4, 21, 22 ; in São Paulo, 4
Carnavalesco, 20, 21
Carreiro, Tião, e Pardinho, 114
Carreiro, Zé, e Carreirinho, 114
Cartola, 23, 34, 46
Carvalho, Beth, 23, 25
Carvalho, Martha Ulhôa de, 48–50
Castro, Max de, 26
Cavalo-marinho, xiii, 71–86, 108, 111, 130, 156; distinguished from *bumba-meu-boi*, 72; in performance, 75–86; performance contexts, 75; performers and audiences, 73–74; present state, 86
Cavaquinho, Nelson, 46
Caymmi, Dorival, 16, 23, 47
Cazes, Henrique, 30
Cearense, Catulo da Paixão, 31
César, Telma, 158
Chitãozinho e Xororó, 119
Choro, xiii, 29–35, 123
Ciata, Tia, 8
Cícero, Padre, 54
Cole, Nat, 44
Comadre Florzinha, 156, 158
Connell, Andrew, 34
Corrêa, Roberto, 110, 115–17
Cosmopolitanism, xii, xiv, 131–58
Costa, Gal, 23, 46, 47, 99
Curto, Rob, 108

Davis, Miles, 132
Demônios da Garoa, 23
Dengue, 134
Dent, Alex, 120
Devotos, 119, 138, 143–48
Diegues, Carlos, 44
DJ Dolores (Hélder Aragão), xiv; and Orchestra Santa Massa, 151–56
Djavan, 22
Dodô and Osmar, 22
Dominguinhos, 99
Donato, João, 43
Donga, 8, 14, 31
Duprat, Rogério, 36, 46

Electrônica, xiv, 6, 151–56
Eller, Cássia, 22, 132, 156
Ellington, Duke, 132

Faces do Subúrbio, 138, 148–51
Fagner, Raimundo, 99
Falamansa, 101, 108
Flores, Raul, e Florêncio, 114
Folia de Reis, 109, 111–12
Forró, xiv, 94–108, 143, 154; etymology, 95; and Northeastern identity, 107–8; *pé-de-serra*, 101; stylized, 101
França, Isaar, 156, 158
Fred04, xvi, 27, 139–44
Frevo, 1, 3, 4
Freyre, Gilberto, 14, 44

Gaita, 126, 130
Galinsky, Philip, xvi, 25, 158
Gallet, Luciano, 14
Garnizé, 148
Gaúcha, Música, xiv, 110, 121–30; nativist movement, 122–24; progressive, 125–30
Gender, xiii, 28; and lyrics of "Trem das Onze," 23; and samba, 11–13; and traditional and popular music in Recife, 156–58; and women in *choro*, 34–35
Getz, Stan, 39, 41, 42
Gil, Gilberto, 23, 46–49, 69, 99
Gilberto, Astrud, 39–41, 45
Gilberto, João, xiii, 23, 37, 39–42, 45, 53, 158
Gilliam, Angela, 13
Gimbel, Norman, 41
"Girl From Ipanema, The," 38–42
Gismonti, Egberto, 69
Gnattali, Radamés, 33, 34, 36
Gomes, Carlos, 36
Gonzaga, Chiquinha, 31, 33, 35
Gonzaga, Luiz, xiv, 80, 95–101, 103–5, 133, 158; and the *baião*, 95, 97; and the invention of the Northeast, 100
Gonzaguinha, 99
Gottschalk, Louis Moreau, 36
Gregory, Jonathan, 10
Grupo de Capoeira Angola Pelourinho, 60–61
Grupo Fundo de Quintal, 25
Grupo Uakti, 69
Guedes, Beto, 49
Guerra Peixe, César, 36
Guineto, Almir, 25
Guitarrada, 70

Helena, Maria, 158
Heleno dos Oito Baixos, 103
Hip-hop, 27

Holanda, Sérgio Buarque de, 14
Horne, Lena, 44
Horta, Toninho, 49

Jabá, 137
Jackson do Pandeiro, 23, 24
Jazz, and *bossa nova*, 40, 44; and "Chiclete com Banana," 24; and *choro*, 31, 34; and samba, 7
Jesus, Clementina de, 23
Jobim, Antonio Carlos, xiii, 37–42, 45, 47, 158
Jovem Guarda, 51

Kayapó-Xikrin, xiii, 63–69
Kenton, Stan, 44
Kessel, Barney, 44
Keti, Zé, 46
KSB, DJ, 148

Lago, Mario, 12
Lambada, 25, 70
Lara, Ivone, 23, 32
Leão, Nara, 46, 46, 47
Leonardo, 122–25
Lewis, J. Lowell, 55, 61
Literatura de cordel, 74
Livingston, Tamara, 33
Lobato, Pio, 70
Lobo, Edu, 46
London, Julie, 44
Lopes, Honorino, 32
Lopes, Nei, 23
Louzeiro, José, 144
Lubambo, Romero, 35
Lucas, Maria Elizabeth, 121–23
Lúcia, Sílvia, 103
Luna, Marcelo, 148
Lyra, Carlos, 38, 46

Ma, Yo-Yo, 32, 33
Macalé, Jards, 23
Maia, Lúcio, 134–37, 142
Malandro, 12
Malfatti, Anita, 14
Mangue movement, 133–44, 155, 158
Maracatu, xiii, xiv, 1, 3, 86–94, 108, 130, 146, 156; difference between *maracatu de baque virado* and *maracatu de baque solto*, 86–87; and globalization, 90; *maracatu rural*, 89–94; *maracatu sambada*, 87–89
Marcelo D2, 27
Massacre, Marcelo, 148
Mastruz com Leite, 101
Mattar, Renata, 156, 158
Medeiros, Anacleto de, 33
Medeiros, Elton, 23
Mendonça, Newton, 38
Menescal, Roberto, 38, 46
Mercury, Daniela, 22
Mestre Ambrósio, 86, 108, 138, 143, 156
Military government (1964–1985), 21, 37, 47, 48, 54
Miranda, Carmen, 17, 18, 45, 158
Miranda, Marlui, 69
Modernism, 15
Modernization, xiv
Monte, Marisa, 53, 132
Monteiro, Jamilson (Mr. Jam), 156
Moraes, Vinícius de, 38, 42, 46
Moura, Paulo, 9, 33
Movimento dos Sem-Terra, 77
Mulata, 13
Mutantes, Os, 46
Mundo Livre S/A, 27, 138–44
Música popular brasileira (MPB), xiii, 48–50

Nação Zumbi, 134–138, 156
Nascimento, Joel, 35
Nascimento, Milton, 48–50, 69, 99
National identity, xii, xiv, 13–17, 54, 158; and Afro-Brazilian culture, 14; and art music, 36; and the *baião*, 95, 100; and *capoeira*, 62; and Carmen Miranda, 45; and *choro*, 29, 34, 35; and Devotos, 147; and jazz, 7; and Milton Nascimento, 49, 50; and media politics, 144; and *música caipira*, 113; and *samba-enredo*, 21; and U.S. influence, 23–24; and Vargas government, 15 and media politics, 144;
Nazareth, Ernesto, 31, 33
Neilton, 144–48
Nelson, Willie, 119
Nunes, Clara, 23

Ogan, Toca, 134
Oiticica, Hélio, 46
Oliveira, Aloysio, 17
Oliven, Ruben George, 12
Olodum, 22
Oni, 148
Orfeu Negro, 20, 37
Ortiz, Fernando, 14
Otto, 152

Pagode, 23–26
Pagodinho, Zeca, 23, 25
Paralamas do Sucesso, 22
Pardo, Juliana, 74
Partido-alto, 25
Pascoal, Hermeto, 35, 132
Patrício, 14
Peixe, Jorge dü, 134–37, 142

Pelé, 44
"Pelo Telefone," 9
Pena Branca e Xavantinho, 114
Pereira dos Santos, Nelson, 44
Pernambuco, João, 31
Perrone, Charles, xvi, 24, 48, 49
Pesce, Lina, 35
Pires, Cornélio, 113
Pixinguinha, 8, 14, 31–33, 35, 158
Possi, Zizi, 23
Powell, Baden, 26, 39, 46
Pupilo, 134

Quarteto em Cy, 43
Queiroga, Lula, 156
Quilombo, 56, 62

Rabeca, 81, 152, 154, 167
Rabello, Luciana, 35
Rabello, Raphael, 35
Raimundos, 143
Ramalho, Elba, 99
Raminho, 102
Rap, xiv, 27, 149
Ratliff, Ben, 135
Regina, Elis, 42
Regional identity, xiii, xiv, 130, 158; and *forró*, 107–8; *gaúcho*, 123, 129; and Luiz Gonzaga, 100; Northeastern, 94, 144
Reily, Suzel Ana, xvi, 111
Reis, Diego, 105
Renato L., xvi
Rian, Bruno, 35
Rian, Déo, 35
Rocha, Glauber, 44
Rodrigues, Jair, 42
Ropni (Raoni), 68
Rosa, Noel, 16

Salustiano, Maciel, 152, 155
Salustiano, Mestre (Manoel), xvi, 74, 156
Samba, xii, 5–28, 32, 39, 50, 54, 123; *escola de samba*, 1, 4–6, 9, 19, 20, 21; "mystery of samba," 13, 14, 27; percussion patterns, 11, 12; *samba-enredo*, 21
Sandroni, Carlos, 12
Sanfona de oito baixos, 101, 103–7; symbolic importance, 104–5; technique, 104
Sargento, Nelson, 23
Saudade, 12
Scheper-Hughes, Nancy, 77–78
Science, Chico, 134–36, 138, 141, 144
Seeger, Anthony, 63
Sepultura, 69
Sertaneja, Música, xiv, 25, 50, 109, 117–21, 130
Sève, Mário, 35
Sheik Tosado, 138
Shorter, Wayne, 49
Siba, xvi, 84, 86, 91–94, 154, 156–57; and *Fuloresta do Samba*, 91
Silva, Bezerra da, 23
Silva, Inácio Lucindo da, xvi, 74
Silva, Luiz Inácio "Lula" da, 119
Silva, Ismael, 9
Silva, Orlando, 16
Silva, Synval, 17
Simon, Paul, 22
Simonal, Wilson, 26
Sinatra, Frank, 42, 43
Sinhô, 8
Soares, Elza, 23
Solberg, Helena, 17
Spielmann, Daniela, 35
Sting, 68, 69

Tamba Trio, 43
Telles, Sylvia, 38
Tiger, 148, 149
Tiso, Wagner, 49
Tormé, Mel, 43
Torres e Florêncio, 118
Tribalistas, 132
Trinta, Joãozinho, 21
Trios elétricos, 22
Tropicália, xiii, 15, 18, 19, 36, 46–48
Trummer, Fábio, 155
Turner, Terence, 63, 68

Valença, Alceu, 99
Vandré, Geraldo, 26
Vanildo de Pombos, 108
Vargas, Getúlio, 15, 17, 20, 54, 62
Vaughan, Sarah, 43
Velha Guarda da Mangueira, 23
Veloso, Caetano, 18, 19, 22, 23, 45–48, 52, 99
Vianna, Hermano, 13, 14, 27
Vidal Giannini, Isabelle, 65
Vidal, Lux Boelitz, 65
Vila, Martinho da, 23
Vila Nova, Ivanildo, 138
Vilar, Gustavo, 86
Villa-Lobos, Heitor, 14, 32, 34, 36, 110
Viola caipira, 115–17, 149
Viola, Paulinho da, 23, 33

World Social Forum, 129–30

Xukuru Indians, 140, 141

Zé, Tom, 23, 46, 47
Zimbo Trio, 42
Zumbi, 56, 62, 134